OUT OF THE BLUE

–OUT OF THE–
BLUE

LIFE ON THE ROAD WITH
MUDDY WATERS

BRIAN BISESI
FOREWORD BY BOB MARGOLIN

University Press of Mississippi / Jackson

The University Press of Mississippi is the scholarly publishing agency of
the Mississippi Institutions of Higher Learning: Alcorn State University,
Delta State University, Jackson State University, Mississippi State University,
Mississippi University for Women, Mississippi Valley State University,
University of Mississippi, and University of Southern Mississippi.

www.upress.state.ms.us

The University Press of Mississippi is a member
of the Association of University Presses.

Library of Congress Cataloging-in-Publication Data

Names: Bisesi, Brian, author. | Margolin, Bob, writer of foreword.

Title: Out of the blue : life on the road with Muddy Waters / Brian Bisesi, foreword by
Bob Margolin.

Other titles: America made music series.
Description: Jackson : University Press of Mississippi, 2024. | Series: American made
music series

Identifiers: LCCN 2023041001 (print) | LCCN 2023041002 (ebook) | ISBN
9781496849120 (hardback) | ISBN 9781496849847 (trade paperback) | ISBN
9781496849809 (epub) | ISBN 9781496849816 (epub) | ISBN 9781496849823 (pdf) |
ISBN 9781496849830 (pdf)
Subjects: LCSH: Muddy Waters, 19151983. | Bisesi, Brian. | Blues musiciansUnited
StatesBiography.
Classification: LCC ML420.M748 B57 2024 (print) | LCC ML420.M748 (ebook) | DDC
782.421643092 [B]dc23/eng/20230920

LC record available at https://lccn.loc.gov/2023041001

LC ebook record available at https://lccn.loc.gov/2023041002

British Library Cataloging-in-Publication Data available

This book is dedicated to the memory of:

Carl and Rosemarie Bisesi
Ola Dixon
Luther "Guitar Junior" Johnson
Joe Willie "Pinetop" Perkins
Calvin "Fuzz" Jones
Willie "Big Eyes" Smith
Joseph Benjamin "J.B." Hutto
Iverson "Louisiana Red" Minter
Joe Berson
Barry Jackson
Victoria "Queen Victoria" Spivey
Muddy Waters

Gone but not forgotten

CONTENTS

PART THREE

ACKNOWLEDGMENTS

Special thanks to Jed Horne, the catalyst for helping me turn memories into serviceable prose. He is a writer who loves the blues, I'm a guitarist and a storyteller. It made for a great collaboration.

Also a thank you to Craig W. Gill, director at the University Press of Mississippi for helping me bring this project to life. He was a pleasure to work with.

Katie Turner, executive assistant at the University Press of Mississippi for her endless patience with me as I tried to navigate all of the forms needed for publication.

Paul Natkin for the cover photo. Scott Shigley for permission to use the Jazz Fest riverboat photo.

Many thanks to the entire staff at the press. I appreciate the hard work you have done to make this happen.

To all of the people who helped me in my musical journey, I appreciate each and every one of you.

And to my dear wife Ann for always being there for me and never complaining about this crazy life I've led in music.

FOREWORD

Of course biographers, music writers, and people who knew Muddy Waters write about him. He is the legendary godfather of electric Chicago blues and a force of nature. His depth and power are unsurpassed. He was musically and personally magnetic. He inspired love and devotion from his worldwide audience and especially from other musicians. He was an original pioneer as a singer, electric and acoustic guitarist, bandleader, songwriter, and influence on his contemporaries and those that came after.

But who was Muddy, the man, beyond the recordings, videos, and interviews that are all we have of him directly since he passed in 1983? Brian Bisesi sheds new light from his unique, direct experience with Muddy. Brian was around him closely and intensively from 1978–80, as a musician and close friend. He was employed by Muddy as a road manager and designated guitar player.

I was one of the other guitar players in Muddy's band since August 1973, before Brian got with us, until June 1980 when . . . Brian will tell you about the tragedy and the aftermath in depth from the inside. I met Brian in the mid-1970s. He was a younger guitar player that shared my love of Muddy's music and we became good friends. He was already a fine and experienced Chicago blues guitar player. I'm finding out now he has excellent recall and talent for imparting his experiences in an engaging and soulful way.

More than any other writing I've seen about Muddy, Brian reveals the daily life from participation and observation on the road with the band—the amazing musical family and brotherhood, the blessings and challenges, our band slang and expressions, and the musical, spiritual experience of being with Muddy on and off the bandstand. I bear witness that Brian is telling it like it was as far as what I saw personally.

Brian saw quirks, grace, and wisdom. He saw much that I didn't see, because he picked up the money at the end of each gig and brought it to Muddy. If Muddy had something to say in the moment, he said it to Brian. He dealt with Muddy's manager but worked for Muddy directly, not the manager. From what I knew of Muddy, Brian's experiences as he relates them now ring true and flesh out events as I remember them.

Stepping back for perspective, this is a book about music and musicians and their lives. Muddy is loved and respected, but he's not famous like the rock stars who idolized him, were drawn to him, and were influenced by him. Yeah, celebrities are interesting. Some are part of Brian's story, but he, they, and I were around Muddy because we love and respect that man and his music. This book will bring you closer in a way that goes beyond biography and history. Thank you, Brian, for bringing me back and telling me more.

BOB MARGOLIN

OUT OF THE BLUE

PART
ONE

NIGHT FLIGHT

In July 1979 I boarded a 747 to Paris from New York. Many of the passengers were jazz and blues musicians bound for festivals across Europe. I was barely out of high school, a young guitarist in love with the blues and traveling with legends. I recognized some faces; many I did not. I just wanted to find my seat and settle in for the long, packed flight ahead.

Thanks to a knuckleheaded travel agent, I was stuck in a middle seat. Bob Margolin, one of Muddy Waters's guitar players, had lucked out with the window seat. To my surprise, the aisle seat was occupied by the great Texas tenor sax man Arnett Cobb. Okay, I was sandwiched into a middle seat, but at least I was in good company.

After climbing to cruising altitude, it was time for beverages. So far, this had been uneventful, a typical night flight to Europe. That was about to change. As the beverage cart made its way to our row, Arnett turned to me and asked what I was drinking. I assumed he was just taking orders. "Gin," I replied. Within a second, he had reached into the cart and retrieved a couple of splits. And in one continuous motion, he deposited the bottles into the seat-back pouch in front of me. Pretty slick, I thought. He then reached into the cart for some drinks for himself. He did this totally undetected by the flight attendant. I sensed Arnett had a mischievous side to him, and that there was more to come. I was right.

A few minutes later he reached into the cart again for more drinks. Only this time the flight attendant caught a glimpse of what he was doing. The attendant said something in French. Arnett just smiled and started in on his drinks. With a raised eyebrow, the attendant placed several straight pins into the top of Arnett's seat cushion. Apparently, the pins were to keep track of how many drinks each passenger had ordered, with payment to be collected later in the flight. Caught in the act, Arnett would be denied the five-finger discount he had been counting on. He came up with another idea: As the beverage cart moved down the aisle, he got up from his seat, started taking the pins out of his and other seats and randomly sticking them in other seats. It looked like his goal was to mess up the flight attendant's pin system, making it impossible for him to know who had how many drinks. It worked! The flight attendant threw up his hands in defeat. Ahh, free drinks! At that moment, I realized two things. Number one, it was probably not the first time Arnett had pulled this prank. Number two, this was going to be an interesting flight.

After a few gin drinks (courtesy of Arnett) and some conversation, I dozed off. I must have been asleep for a couple of hours when I was awakened by the sound of a saxophone coming from the back of the plane. I opened my eyes and looked around. The plane was mostly dark, but an overhead reading light spotlit the face of the sax player just below it. The scene was haunting, surreal, and beautiful. I watched him for a few moments. Only as he reached up and switched off the light did I realize who he was: Sonny Stitt, the great bebop player. I began to wonder, was this a dream? No, it couldn't be, because I was definitely awake now. I looked at the man sleeping in the seat to my left. It was definitely Bob Margolin. And in the seat to my right, was the gentleman who had introduced himself to me as Arnett Cobb, also asleep. With no one to talk to, I began to wonder how the hell I got here.

I've been asked the question many times: How did you ever get hooked up with Muddy Waters? I always tell people I made three rights. I was in the right place, at the right time, and I played the right thing, a guitar. And that's how it happened.

Chapter 2

RIGHT PLACE

It all began a year earlier on March 14, 1978, at a club in West Orange, New Jersey, called Creation. I was a regular at whatever shows Muddy was doing in the New York area or around Boston. I hadn't made it to Boston the previous weekend because of a big snowstorm. So, I was not aware that Luther "Guitar Junior" Johnson, a vocalist as well as a guitarist, had slipped on the ice and gone back to Chicago to recover from his fall. I knew all the guys in the band and Muddy too, but to them I was just a dedicated fan.

No one except Bob Margolin, Muddy's other guitar player, knew that I played. On tour with Muddy, Bob had seen me in Boston with a group that included guitarist Ronnie Earl—he was still known as Ronnie Horvath back then—bassist Michael "Mudcat" Ward, drummer Ola Dixon, Jim McKaba on piano, and Danny Russo, a great harmonica player Muddy was fond of. Just ahead of showtime in West Orange, Bob approached me: "Would you like to sit in tonight?" I knew from being around the band that a lot of people would bother Muddy and ask him if they could sit in. It was mostly harmonica players. (I always felt bad for Jerry Portnoy, Muddy's harmonica player, because there always seemed to be someone asking to sub for him.)

I never would have asked to sit in because, number one, I didn't want to bother Muddy, and, number two, I had only been playing guitar for a few years. I started off as a drummer when I was a kid. Eventually, my parents (and the neighbors) got fed up with all the banging, and the drums had to go. That's when I set my sights on my brother Ralph's Fender bass. If the banging was more than they could stand, my parents didn't seem to mind the twanging, and I think Ralph got

5

a laugh out of it, because the bass was as big as me. I also knew how to play a little bit of guitar because Ralph's friend Burt Miller had taught me some chords and basics. I didn't really get serious about it until the midseventies—only about two years before fate, in the person of McKinley "Muddy Waters" Morganfield, intervened in my life. Fortunately, what I had been playing were mostly Muddy's songs. Plus, I had seen Muddy's show so many times that I knew it by heart.

I had no trouble accepting Bob's offer to sit in. Yes, sir! He told me that there were only two guitars available, his and Muddy's. But he had a plan. The band always opened the set with three instrumental numbers before Muddy joined in. I would play the three opening numbers with the band, Bob said. He would play Muddy's guitar, and I would play his. Then when it was time to introduce Muddy, we would switch guitars. "I'll hand Muddy his, you hand me mine, then get off the stage." Yes, sir!

I had been turning up at Muddy's shows and listening to his records for years, but nothing had prepared me for the rush that came with being onstage with him. The power of his voice and the tightness of a road-hardened band took everything to a level that I had never experienced before. As a young guy growing up in Glen Rock, a small New Jersey town not far from New York City, I had dreamed only of one day meeting Muddy Waters. Actually playing with him was just a fantasy. When both of those things came together, I had to pinch myself to make sure it was actually happening.

As I took my place on the stage, I found myself wishing it could have happened later when I'd be a stronger player, but that wasn't in the cards. It was bound to be downhill after this, I told myself. As I left the stage after those three opening numbers, I passed Muddy walking on. He grabbed my arm, looked me straight in the eye, and said, "I want to talk to you after the show."

I went back to my table, and sat down with a couple of friends. Their minds were blown and they wanted to celebrate. They had just watched a pal—this twenty-two-year-old Italian dude from the Jersey suburbs—play with a Deep South blues legend named Muddy

Waters. I tried to hose them down. "I pissed off the old man," I said. "I must have really fucked up. Muddy told me to come and talk to him after the show. He's never said that to me before and I've been going to see him for a few years now." I sat there completely bummed out for the rest of the set. When it was over, I wondered whether I should just leave and never go to one of Muddy's shows again. Instead, out of respect for him, I went back to the dressing room to take my medicine. I found Muddy sitting at a table in the corner of the room. "Come over here," he said. "I want to talk to you."

I walked over and he told me to sit down. Muddy was sipping champagne. He put his glass down and said, "How come you never told me you play guitar?" I replied, "I didn't want to be one of those people that comes around and bothers you." I told Muddy it was enough that he and all the guys just let me hang out with them.

"Well, you play my style," Muddy replied.

"I love your style, that's what I'm trying to play," I said. At which point he blew what was left of my mind: "When the guys do the next show, why don't you play the opening songs with them?"

So, I did it again. I joined the band for the three opening songs—this time Calvin Jones and Pinetop Perkins did some vocals—and as I was exiting the stage, I passed Muddy standing in the wings. Once again, he said: "I want to talk to you after the show."

I was back in the audience when it dawned on me that Guitar Junior still hadn't rejoined Muddy's band. I'm thinking to myself: wouldn't it be great if Muddy actually asked me to fill in for Junior (as he was known to Muddy and other members of the band) until he's back? That would be a lifetime dream come true: to play with Muddy's band even if it's just for a little while. I quickly realized I shouldn't be thinking like that—least of all about a guy I would partner and tour with a few years later after Muddy fired the whole band. But, what if?

The end of the night came, I went back into the dressing room and Muddy called me over to where he was sitting. He got right to the point: "You got a guitar?"

I told him I had one at home. The next words out of his mouth floored me, "Do you want to play with my band tomorrow night?" I said, "Sure, I'd love to play with your band tomorrow night." Muddy instructed me to be there at 9:00 p.m. and to bring my guitar (the show didn't actually start until 10:00 p.m.). "You can use Junior's amp."

The guys in the band seemed comfortable with the idea of me sitting in and happy for me that Muddy was on board. They all wanted to see how I would do the next night. It was getting late and at 6:00 a.m. I had to be at my day job in Montvale, New Jersey, doing interior landscaping for Everett Conklin & Company, mostly in New York City office buildings. I spent the whole workday trying to wrap my head around what had happened the night before with Muddy. It was surreal: In a few hours, I was going to be playing with his band! Since I was going to go to the gig right from work, I had my guitar and clothes in my car, back at the nursery. I finished my day job about 4:00 in the afternoon and headed off to West Orange. I was there, dressed in a denim vest and matching slacks—there was no dress code for the band—and ready to play by 6:00 p.m. Three hours early!

Muddy and the band showed up a little before 9:00 p.m. "Oh, you're here early," Muddy said. "That's good, you're on time, I like that." Being on time turned out to be a really big deal with Muddy. Muddy was always on time, and you damn well better be on time, too. I played the entire show with the band that night, two sets, and Muddy's sets were always about an hour long. Muddy gave me a lot of room to play. He let me do a lot of solos and play fills and chords behind his vocals. I noticed him looking at me quite often during the show, he was clearly checking me out. In between sets he told me he really liked the chords and fills. "You get in there, then get out of the way before I start singing. I like that." What a thrill, I was being complimented by Muddy Waters!

I played the second set and I'm happy to report that everything went right. Afterward, I went into the dressing room to pack my things and say thank you and goodnight to everyone. When I made my way over to Muddy he stood up, reached into his pocket and pulled out a huge wad of cash.

Muddy: "How much do you want for playing with my band tonight?"

My first night playing with Muddy, March 15, 1978 (Creation, West Orange, NJ).

Me: "All the money in your pocket wouldn't pay for what you gave me tonight."

Muddy asked me again, "How much do you want? I'll pay you what you want." I said, "I don't want anything. I just want to thank you, it's the greatest night of my life. I got to play with you." Muddy looked bewildered and said, "You don't want any money?" I said, "No, this one's on me."

Muddy stuffed the roll of money back in his pocket. Then he looked at me and said, "Do you want to play with my band? This can't be for long, because you know Junior, right? Junior didn't do anything wrong, Junior just had a little accident. As soon as he's well, he's coming back."

I told Muddy I understood the situation and that I loved the way Junior played and sang. Those were big shoes to fill, and I sure couldn't fill them. But I let Muddy know that I wouldn't mind hanging around for a while. At that point Muddy asked me if I had a day job? I told him I did. He told me they had some gigs coming up and the next one was in Nashville. "I would like you to come with us," he said, "but I don't like to take anybody away from their day job." I told Muddy there wouldn't be a problem. My boss was really great, I said, and my job would still be there when I got back.

Muddy and me after the show (March 15, 1978). Photo by Ola Dixon.

Now pianist Pinetop Perkins piped up. He was sitting within ear-shot of our conversation. "Go ahead, Muddy. Ask him to go with us, ask him." Muddy asked me one more time if I was sure about my day job not being a problem? I reassured him again that it was not a problem. He responded with words that would change my life forever, "You want to go to Nashville?" I said, "I'd love to go to Nashville." He replied, "All right, you talk to Willie ['Big Eyes' Smith] and see what time the boys are leaving. You meet them at the hotel in New York and I'll see you in Nashville."

I have Bob Margolin to thank for suggesting to Muddy that I sit in for Guitar Junior on that fateful Jersey club date in 1978. And I'll be forever indebted to Pinetop Perkins for speaking out when Muddy was hesitant about taking me away from my day job. Pinetop gave Muddy the little push he needed to take me on the road. Thanks again, Pinetop Perkins! A week filling in for Junior turned into several months. And once Muddy got word that Junior was well enough to return, he would ask me to stay on as his right-hand guy on the road. It was an incredible piece of luck that became the next two-and-a-half years of my life.

Chapter 3

RIGHT SOUND

Aside from the chords and fills that he mentioned, what I think caught Muddy's attention the first night I sat in with the band was that I played his style of raw, hard-edged Chicago blues, not B.B. King–style blues. Not that Muddy had anything but respect for B.B. King.

In moving to Chicago, Muddy had basically taken the acoustic Delta style that he grew up with and amplified it. You needed amps to be heard in the noisy Chicago clubs. And later Muddy added more instruments—the two guitars, bass, drums, piano, harmonica—the blueprint for the classic Chicago blues sound of the 1950s, which he would use throughout his career. The Stones and other British groups—the Yardbirds, to name another—picked up on this format, sometimes minus the harmonica or piano.

B.B. King played a more Memphis style of blues, a more "uptown" style, as Muddy would say. It was more sophisticated, it had a jazzy element to it. And usually horns as well. Bobby Bland and Little Milton were in B.B.'s groove. Of course, the different styles blended together. But those styles and the musicians who played that kind of blues had Muddy's deepest respect. I learned that after being on shows with some of them as I traveled with Muddy.

I think what Muddy liked about my playing when I sat in the first time was that I was firmly rooted in the Chicago style of blues.

The second night that I played with Muddy for the whole show, he saw something else that made him comfortable having me around. He saw that I could use a capo (he called it a "clamp"), which was a big part of the way he played guitar. As serious guitar geeks will know, the capo allows you to get that open-string sound, like you are playing a pattern in the key of E. Muddy's approach was to play his bass patterns, like he was playing in E, but by moving the capo up or down the neck he could play the same pattern in F, G, or A.

I learned that Muddy would not always call out what key he was playing in. You had to watch him to see whether he moved the capo up or down the neck.

For the key of C he would leave the capo on the third fret and use the A string as the bottom instead of the E string; this is how he played "Kansas City," for example.

Those were basically his keys, C, G, A, and F, never the flats. He always started the show with the capo on the third fret (key of G), then moved it up to the fifth fret for the key of A, or down to the first fret for the key of F. If he was tired or his voice felt tight, he would immediately slide the capo toward the headstock and play in F.

He didn't play guitar at all on "Got My Mojo Working" (key of E). Instead he would signal to Pinetop Perkins to start the song on the piano. Muddy would come in on the vocals.

When the guys in the band heard that I would be traveling with them for a while, there was one exception to the warm welcome they gave me: for all he had done to get me onstage with Muddy that first time, Bob Margolin seemed a little disappointed to learn that I was coming along to Nashville.

With Junior out on sick leave, maybe Bob had wanted to finish the tour with just him and Muddy playing guitars. And a few musicians not with the band got a little pissed at me when they heard Muddy had taken me on, if only for a while. I don't know if it came from jealousy, or if it was because of me being so young and inexperienced (which I was), or both. Since I had auditioned for the gig at those shows in West Orange, I never felt like it was just handed to me without merit. Whatever. I wasn't going to turn down an opportunity like this. I would always say to anyone who had a problem with me accepting Muddy's offer, "What would you have done? Would you have turned down the gig?" No one ever answered me.

After a while, the early tension with Bob went away. I owe him for coaching me on how to weave two guitars together on the turnarounds, with the guitars going in different directions, one ascending, one descending. Muddy called this weaving of two guitars together "filling in the cracks." It was something he and Jimmy Rogers used to do in his era as the guitarist in Muddy's early 1950s band. Another example: Keith Richards and Ronnie Wood of the Rolling Stones use the technique very effectively to this day.

Jerry Portnoy tipped me to the way Muddy liked you to send it back to him after a solo. Muddy wanted a soft send-back. You needed to lower the volume before he'd start singing. In other words he wanted you to serve it back to him gently, not throw it at him hard.

Pinetop Perkins also had a bit of advice that stayed with me: "Be where they ain't." It was very good counsel. Everybody gets their moment in a blues band, even a seven-piece band. That meant a lot of time trying to keep from stepping on anybody's toes or crowding them out.

That night, after the gig in New Jersey, I went home and packed my suitcase. I actually had not cleared the Nashville trip with my boss, Everett Conklin. I knew he would be okay with me taking a couple of weeks off. He knew who Muddy was, and I'm sure it helped that his son was a guitar player, studying at the Berklee School of Music in Boston. My partner on my day job had gone out to the gig the previous night and had seen me sit in with Muddy. So my boss had already caught wind of this development before I arrived for work that morning at 6:00 a.m.

I went straight into his office to tell him that I was going to be away for a while, a once-in-a-lifetime opportunity. Everett was thrilled. "That is wonderful," he said. I told him I would be back in a couple weeks. He was skeptical: "No, I don't think I'll be seeing you back here again. Good luck to you." Turns out he was right; I never went back.

Chapter 4

REALITY CHECK

Most road trips began from Chicago. Everyone would meet either at Muddy's house outside of the city or at Willie Smith's place, which was Muddy's old house on the rough-and-tumble South Side. Bob Margolin, Jerry Portnoy, and me—the white guys in the group—stayed in a more integrated neighborhood and typically would get together at the hotel and take a cab to Willie's place. Safety in numbers. Willie would already have one of the vehicles waiting for us to depart. We'd throw our bags into it and, if there was time to kill, go inside. For some reason, we always seemed to leave around midnight, the official departure time. First stop was to pick up Pinetop Perkins, who we would sometimes find working on a car in front of his house when we arrived. Then we would head off to Harold's Chicken Shack.

Harold's Chicken Shack was our official go-to source for road-worthy cuisine at the start of any trip: fried chicken, of course, but also gizzards, liver, and other, more mysterious parts that I was not all that familiar with. We'd order from the sidewalk through a bulletproof window. After a short wait, the food would be handed back out to us in a greasy brown bag reeking of the Shack's "special sauce." Back inside the vehicle, the guys would lay the bags on the seats and start "greasin' down." The food smells, mixed with clouds of cigarette smoke, would quickly crowd out whatever fresh air we arrived with. With a long day of travel ahead of me, I was never too tempted to overload on bird, but the guys really looked forward to starting off with a taste of home, so I never minded the stop.

This trip, my first after sitting in for Guitar Junior in New Jersey, was different. For one thing, it started in New York, not Chicago.

After telling my boss at the landscaping company, that I was going to be gone for a while, I went into the city to meet the guys at the Century Paramount Hotel on West 46th Street. The band traveled in two Chevy Suburbans. Muddy always flew if the next gig was more than a hundred miles away. I was informed upon arrival that since I was filling in for Junior, that meant also taking his place behind the wheel. It was part of the gig. Willie Smith would be driving the other, like he always did. The band's routine was that each driver was expected to "burn a tank," as they put it, terminology that was new to me. What it meant was that I was expected to drive until the tank was half-full, which was about two hundred miles. Then, they would look for a gas station, preferably a Union 76. We'd gas up, get a bite to eat, roam the gift shop, and change drivers if one of us got too tired.

I was so wired from thinking about what was happening that I got in the vehicle and just kept driving. From New York down to Nashville is about nine hundred miles. It took us about twenty hours to make the trip, and I drove almost the entire way. The guys were impressed. Willie had been considered the king of the road. He was able to drive endless miles without needing to rest, so I was up against stiff competition. I started to hear some of the guys talking about me: "That Brian, he's a driver, this guy can really drive." When we got to Nashville, Muddy (who had already flown in) wanted to know how I did and word got back to him that I drove my ass off the whole way down. My first gig on the road with Muddy was also the first time I got paid. At the end of the two-nighter (March 17–18, 1978), Muddy reached into his pocket and handed me $180. He then asked if I had ever made that much playing my guitar? I gave him the answer he was waiting for: "No." He looked at me and smiled, then kind of laughed. He knew he had me. I was thrilled because I had been busting my ass on a ten-hour-a-day landscaping job that started at 6:00 a.m. and paid $80 a week. I would eventually learn that the pay wasn't as sweet as it seemed, especially for the guys in the band who were supporting families.

At that time the pay for a one-nighter was $130. Two nights: $180. Three nights: $250. For full week, the pay topped out at $270—unless we were overseas, in which case we got a flat $600 a week, hotel room included. Stateside, though, we were responsible for all our own expenses—hotel, food, taxes—and the cost was on you to get to Chicago or wherever a tour's first date had you playing. A couple of the guys (not me) got an extra $25 per gig for driving. But, hey! I wasn't complaining. Far from it. Being young and single, it felt like I had hit the motherlode. I was going to enjoy the ride for however long it might last.

Muddy liked to tag people with nicknames and immediately coined one for me. He started calling me Driver. I heard him ask some of the guys, "Can Driver burn a tank?" And they would reply, "He can burn a lot of tanks." The guys in the band also started calling me Driver. "Hey, Driver!" That's how that happened. The fact is, Muddy didn't really know my name when I first started working for him. He thought my name was Ryan. So for the first couple of months, he would introduce me by announcing, "On my left, playing the guitar, this is Ryan!" I didn't have the nerve to correct him.

One night, we're sitting around in the dressing room and Muddy heard one of the guys call my name. "Hey, Brian!" Muddy looked at me and said, "Wait a minute, I thought your name was Ryan." And I said to him, "Well, it's Brian, it's Ryan with a B in front of it." Muddy unloaded on me, "Why didn't you tell me that?" I said, "Well, I didn't want to say anything to you." Muddy was now clearly pissed off. "You should have told me, you let me stand up there and introduce you by the wrong name. What the hell is wrong with you!" So, from that day on Muddy knew that there was a B in front of "Ryan's" name.

By the time I started traveling with the band in 1978, CB radios, the prime mode of communication for truckers, were getting popular in some passenger vehicles, too, including ours. We'd communicate with each other about road conditions, speed traps, or accidents ahead. Everybody had a handle. Willie Smith was the Culligan Man (or the Chicken Man). Bob Margolin was the Wolfman, Jerry Portnoy was the Whistler, Calvin "Fuzz" Jones was Po' Tom, Guitar Junior was the

Windy City Kid, Muddy was the Big Dog, and his stepson, Charles Williams, who was traveling with the band when I started, was Bang Bang. Pinetop Perkins? Well, he was Pinetop.

On my first trip with the band, as soon as I got into the vehicle Willie Smith asked me: "What's your handle?"

I didn't have one. I had to think fast. The first thing that came to mind was "Little Boy Blue," the song made famous by Delta blues legend, Robert Lockwood Jr. (stepson of the great Robert Johnson). "I'll be Little Boy Blue," I said. They all seemed to like that, maybe because, at twenty-two, I was the youngest.

Sometimes we would be on the same channel as the truckers, but they had a language we were not really fluent in. Other times we would pick a channel that nobody else was on so we could communicate with each other in private—unless one of them found their way onto our channel and was listening in.

Truckers used all kinds of different codes, also called "checks," to communicate with each other on the road, and we had some, too. One that they could never figure out was "reality check." We'd be traveling down the highway and one of the guys in the band would call for a reality check. It would go something like this: "Breaker 1–9 for a reality check." That was our code for some smoke, a joint. One time—actually more than one time—someone would call for a reality check and a trucker listening in would want to know more about this mysterious check. "Reality check? What the hell kind of check is that, boy?"

Muddy would occasionally ride with the band on trips that weren't too long. On the highway, he liked to use the CB radio and when he did, he had a huge voice. Typically, he would use it to call out for Willie Smith, or "Little Dog," as he dubbed him. Muddy didn't use trucker lingo, "breaker 1–9" or any of that. He would just grab the mike and blurt out, "Big Dog to Little Dog, Big Dog to Little Dog."

Willie Smith would sometimes ignore Muddy's call, especially if they had been in an argument earlier that day. So Muddy would just call again, a little louder. "Big Dog to Little Dog, Big Dog to Little Dog." When that didn't work, Muddy would try again, a little louder and with a different handle. "Big Dog to the Chicken Bone. Big Dog to the

Chicken Bone." (He never used Willie's other handles, the Chicken Man or the Culligan Man.)

If Willie Smith still didn't respond, Muddy would get really pissed off and start yelling: "Willie pick up the phone! What the hell is wrong with you, pick up the phone!" Finally, Willie would answer. This was not exactly trucker CB lingo. Not even close. I'm sure we raised a lot of eyebrows with our CB talk!

Chapter 5

MOTHERFUCKER

Playing with Muddy Waters wasn't always sweetness and light. Not for me, not for any of us. The first time I got to see Muddy play up close was at a club in New York City called the Bottom Line, a venue in the Village. He really didn't much like the Bottom Line, I later figured out, not because of the club, but because it was where you played for the industry people and the pay was very low. Before the show he would tell the band, "Tonight I work for you," because it cost him to play there. After we got paid, he wasn't going to make a nickel. But he knew he had to do it.

Anyway, it was at the Bottom Line—I'm still in the audience, not yet on the bandstand—that I noticed something. After he thanked the crowd, he looked over his shoulder at the band, covered his mouth with the back of his hand and said something. I couldn't be sure, but it looked like Willie Smith, the drummer, was on the receiving end. What was he saying? On one of my first nights playing with Muddy I found out. What Muddy had to say was this: "Motherfucker!"

Maybe Willie wasn't hitting the backbeat hard enough, or maybe he had dragged the tempo a little bit. I didn't know, but I was shocked.

Willie wasn't the only one of us who came in for a scolding now and then.

If you've seen videos of the band, you might have noticed Muddy eyeballing Jerry Portnoy, the harmonica player. Jerry was a regular target of Muddy's grief: "You're killing me!" was one comment I overheard him say to his harpist.

My honeymoon period came to an end a couple of weeks into the tour: "Time, motherfucker, time," Muddy snarled at me from behind the back of his hand. Nothing can prepare you for being on the receiving end of one of Muddy's cutting remarks. I was crushed, I didn't know what to do. I was afraid to play a note after that. I just froze.

Luckily, Fuzz Jones, Muddy's bass player, was standing at my side and saw what was happening. In a fatherly way he turned to me and said, "Just stay with me, stay with me, son. Play with me, don't let that bother you." He calmed me down and got me back into the right groove.

To be on the receiving end of Muddy's wrath was something I never wanted to experience again. I had the utmost respect for the man and his music. And fortunately, it didn't happen to me often. Muddy would usually wait until after the set was over to tell you what was bothering him.

But, hey, there was a bright side to this rite of passage. I was now a member of a unique club: the Muddy-Waters-Called-Me-a-Motherfucker club.

Another thing I learned early on was that being on the road with a band that mixed whites and blacks could make for problems with the authorities. During one of the first trips I made with Muddy's band we were playing at Antone's, in Austin, Texas. Antone's was one of Muddy's favorite gigs—also the band's. Clifford Antone, the owner, had the deepest respect for all of the older bluesmen (and women). And the crowd response at his club was as good as it gets. Antone made everyone feel at home, even the new kid on the block—me! The gig at Antone's was for several nights (April 18–22, 1978), and when that was over we had a one-nighter on April 23 at a club in Houston, Liberty Hall. Since Houston was only a few hours away, it was decided that we would stay in Austin and not have to change hotels. Muddy wanted no part of this and flew to Houston.

We drove from Austin to Houston, did the gig, loaded up the equipment, and got back in the Suburbans, me driving one, and Willie Smith the other. This is what the band called a "hit and run."

We reached Austin in the wee small hours. I pulled up in front of the hotel, bleary-eyed from all that driving. We just wanted to get to our rooms and get some sleep. Willie had pulled into the parking garage, but I parked in front of the hotel so the guys could grab their instruments and not have to walk too far to the hotel entrance. I was about to find out what a bad idea this was.

Since I was dog tired, as I turned off the ignition I handed the keys to Jerry Portnoy so he could unlock the rear door (the vehicle did not have power locks) and start unloading our gear. I was completely unaware of a vehicle that had pulled up behind me.

I stepped out to help with the guitars and walked right into a policeman. A very tall policeman. A cop so tall that his gun, for a short dude like me, was at eye level. I was greeted with these words, "Boy, you going to jail. Move this vehicle! You can't park there."

Before I could say anything, he repeated the threat: "You going to jail." I tried to get the keys from Jerry who had made his way over to where I was standing with this crazed cop. Everything seemed to be moving in slow motion. Jerry had a look of disbelief on his face. I kept looking at that gun. It seemed possible that this asshole cop might just kill me.

It seemed like the cop's biggest problem as we rolled up to the front of the hotel was that he was going to have to pull around us. I had sort of messed up his plan. By stopping by the curb, I posed a threat to his dignity and self-esteem, I guess. He was determined to just keep going straight, not swerve around the Suburban and keep going. I guess that's what it was all about. The fact that we had Illinois plates and were racially mixed didn't help, either.

Somehow I was able to get the keys from Jerry and the cop got back into his vehicle. I was a nervous wreck as I started the Suburban. I knew I was being watched, and that I better be careful not to make a wrong move. I put the Chevy in drive and made my way to the parking garage, which was only about a quarter of a block away. As I started to turn into the garage, I could see the police car in my rearview mirror. The cop was right on my tail. I needed to stop and get a ticket to get into the garage. Because of the size of the Suburban, the tail end was still partially in the street as I grabbed the ticket and, of course, the cop was not going to turn his wheel even a little bit and pull around me. He did not budge until I was all the way into the garage. I found a parking slip and made my way into the hotel lobby, still shaking. Fuzz took one look at me and said, "Are you okay?" I said, "Yeah, that cop scared the hell out of me." Fuzz's next words stayed with me: "Well, son, now you have a little idea of how we were treated in the South when I was growing up." I'll never forget that.

But it wasn't just the South. Another time we got hassled was way up by the Canadian border. Going into Canada never seemed to be a problem. They were usually pretty nice to us. Coming back was when we might run into trouble. I remember one time when we were returning from Montreal. We pulled into the checkpoint and were asked to park the vehicle and get out. The guards took us inside and told us to sit down. I smelled trouble; what came next shocked me. One by one the US border agents took each of the band's Black members into a back room and strip-searched them—even the elderly Pinetop Perkins. Jerry, Bob, and I, the white guys, were left alone and not searched. When we stood up to protest the harassment of the others, we were told to sit down and shut up. Blacks, I came to realize, were subject to humiliation like this everywhere. And these were grown men, not kids with pockets full of weed.

A few years later—by then I was touring in a mixed band with Guitar Junior—the same thing happened to us. They pulled us into custody and US border agents strip-searched us. That was one of the ugly sides of touring. I don't know what it's like today, but I doubt it's a whole lot better.

The flip side of that ugliness, one of the really great things about Muddy's band, was that everybody got along really well. Most of the time. It was a family kind of feeling; we had to look out for each other. We traveled a lot of highway together. Sure, there would be times when people just got on each other's nerves. Everyone came out of the bag at someone at some point, me included. The road will do that to you. It's equal opportunity, everybody gets a turn. At some point, somebody's going to get pissed off at somebody. That's just one of the downsides when you're out there riding the highway 50,000 miles a year. That's a lot of time to spend cooped up together.

On my first trip with the band (March 16, 1978), as I settled into the driver's seat Jerry Portnoy turned to me and said, "Welcome to your new home, you're going to spend a lot of time in it." He was right. This was a hard-travelin' band. A local gig was considered anything under a thousand miles. To be in Chicago one night, pack up after the gig and leave for Boston was not unusual, another hit and run. One of my favorites was the time we flew from Chicago to West Palm Beach for an afternoon show at a Florida festival (March 25, 1979). Immediately after the show we went right back to the airport, flew to Chicago, then got into the Suburbans and drove to Tucson, Arizona! It was tough. Nerves would fray. Sometimes, if you just looked at somebody the wrong way, they would snap at you. But then it would be over and done with. This was, after all, just another day on the road. When someone had something to say that was bothering them, they would go ahead and say it and be done with it. That went for everyone, except maybe Fuzz Jones and Pinetop Perkins. They were both really beautiful people, who never seemed to get mad about anything. I don't know how they did it. If something was bothering them, they kept it to themselves.

Drummer Willie Smith was the peacemaker. Before a big tour, especially one that was going to take us overseas, he would gather all of us together. "I want everyone to shake hands before we get on the plane," he'd say. "Whatever we say to each other, whatever I say to you, whatever anybody says to anybody, we didn't mean it. Let's all shake hands because we're all friends." Overseas tours were grueling, a different country every day. None of us ate right or got enough sleep and before long we'd get out of whack and on each other's nerves. There was wisdom in Willie's ritual. He wanted everyone to remain friends throughout the tour and, most of all, after the tour when we returned home. And mostly it worked!

Chapter 6

RIBS À LA MUDDY

Muddy's house in Illinois was in a little village outside Chicago called Westmont, maybe half an hour west of the Loop. Sometimes I'd go by there before a road trip or after one, and I'd usually find Muddy in the kitchen, the center of his domain. Everything revolved around the kitchen. Sometimes he'd be cooking. With a bottle of champagne handy, more often he'd be sitting at the kitchen table by the window, his favorite spot. From there he could survey all the goings-on inside the house and what his dogs were up to in the backyard. The stove was to his left, and the window to his right. It also gave him a view down the hallway to the front door, so he knew who was coming in or going out. And when the weather was good, there was the swimming pool in the backyard and he could keep tabs on that, too.

I was at Muddy's house one time when he was cooking short ribs of beef. He was proud of his short ribs. He'd talk about how tender they were, how they just fell off the bone. Well, I was about to find out if it was true. When I arrived, things were already well underway. He had some pots and pans going on the stove. One for the ribs, one for the greens, one for the pinto beans. And he had some cornbread in the oven. A lot of times when Muddy was cooking, if somebody was around, he would get you to go over and stir a pot for him. He'd sit there watching you, then get up every once in a while to taste and season the food.

I guess I timed this visit just right because everything was almost ready when I arrived. Muddy told me to get a plate. I could tell he wanted to see my reaction to the ribs he had told me so much about and, after all the talk, I was looking forward to finally getting a taste.

I put some ribs on my plate, some pinto beans, some greens, and cornbread. All nice and neat, each in its place on the plate. So, I've got my little plate and I sit down and start to eat. Meanwhile, Muddy has loaded up a plate for himself. He sits down at the table and watches me eat. I knew he was about to make some kind of comment. I continued to work my way through the plate with a fork in one hand and some cornbread in the other. I'm thinking, Muddy wants me to tell him again how great these ribs are—and yes, indeed, they did fall off the bone. "Real good," I said.

Muddy kept looking at me, then finally he had a question: "Is this really the way you eat?" I didn't know where he was going with that, so I just said, yeah. Out of curiosity I asked, "Why? How do you do it?" He must have been hoping I'd ask. "I'll show you the way I do it," he said. First he took the ribs and knocked the meat off of the bones, then he took his cornbread and crumbled it over his plate. Then he started mixing everything all together—the greens, the pinto beans, the meat and the cornbread—until it was more or less mush. I'm watching him do this, and he knows he's got my attention big time. "This is the way we do it down in the country," he said, picking up his fork. "Bet you never seen that before." And I said, "No, never seen that one."

Muddy had a really healthy appetite. Sometimes after a gig he'd ask me or Willie Smith to drive him to a Pancake House or a diner and sit with him. He'd order eggs with a double side of bacon, which used to kind of freak me out. And sometimes he would order pancakes too. Muddy loved pancakes. I couldn't imagine trying to get to sleep after eating all that, but he did. And if there wasn't a Pancake House nearby, we'd have to drive around until we found one. If we were in Europe, forget it: no Pancake Houses. But in the states back then you could usually find something, a Howard Johnson's or a Denny's. (The latter was not one of Muddy's favorites because, as he put it, "they can mess up a glass of water.") Sometimes after a show Muddy would ask the whole band to come with him to a Pancake House. Most of the guys just wanted to go to bed, but Muddy liked to have a full stomach before he lay down, and he had very definite ideas about the best way to fill it up.

I sat with Muddy for a lot of meals when we were on the road. If it was dinner, he loved New York strip steaks, always well done. He would often pull little salt and pepper shakers out of his airplane carry-on bag and bring them into the restaurant. Once the waiter brought the food, he didn't like waiting. If there were no salt and pepper shakers on the table, he would reach into his pocket and pull out his own.

At the end of the meal, Muddy would usually grab the check and tell me to leave the tip. He was very generous that way. He also appreciated it when someone picked up the tab for him. Sometimes I had to be a little creative. With the waiter about to drop the check on the table, I'd try to divert Muddy's attention, usually to a nice-looking woman in the room. As he turned to look at her, I would grab the check and slip away to pay it. I would look back and see him laughing. "Pretty slick," he'd say. "Okay, I'll leave the tip."

If we were having breakfast in the South, he loved that country ham. He used to say to me that after eating country ham, all he wanted was a glass of water because he didn't want to spoil the taste of the ham. If I grabbed the breakfast check, he'd bust my chops. "I buy you steak dinners and you buy me some eggs." I knew he was just messing with me. By the way, with Muddy and the band, if you were going to have eggs for breakfast, you were going to "bust some eggs." Pinetop Perkins baffled many a waitress with some terminology of his own. When they asked how he wanted his eggs, he'd say, "Rake 'em." That meant scrambled.

Chapter 7

COUNTRY MILES

One of Willie Smith's favorite expressions was, "Well, it's the same thing, don't really make no difference, same thing." Muddy used to pick up on that all the time and he got a big kick out of it.

After the Austin dates at Antone's our next stop was El Paso. I pulled out a map as we were about to leave, to figure out the best route. Willie had it in his head that he did not want to take the Interstate. Willie liked back roads, country roads. That's where I learned about "a country mile." "Well, you know, a country mile isn't like a regular mile. It's a little longer than a regular mile." Some of the guys in the band who grew up in the country would say that to me.

I looked carefully at the map, and sure enough Willie had found a route that would get us to El Paso entirely on back roads. I took the map and showed the most direct route to Willie, so he could compare his plan vs. taking the Interstate. I liked to think I could read a map pretty well. If we took the Interstate, we'd get there a lot sooner, I told him.

He looked at me and said, "Well, it's the same thing, it don't really make no difference as long as we get there. It's the same thing, I want to go this way."

I pleaded with him: "Willie, it's going to take us a lot longer. Those are country miles."

Forget about pleading with Willie. When his mind was made up, you weren't going to get through to him. I tried again, tracing the route on the map with my finger. "Willie, look, we can get there hours sooner if we just go this way."

It's one of the few times I remember Willie ever getting mad at me. "My mind's made up, and this is the way we're going."

Willie was really sweet, really kind, and I had a great friendship with him. But when his mind was made up, there was no changing it. Muddy often used Willie's expression whenever it would fit: "Well, it's the same thing, it don't really make no difference." Between Willie and Muddy, they got a lot of mileage out of that one. Twelve hours later, we reached El Paso, completing what would have been a nine-hour drive on the Interstate.

About five weeks into the tour we reached San Francisco, a club called the Old Waldorf. Charlie Musselwhite was also on the bill. Muddy was very fond of Charlie and was delighted that the great singer/harmonica player was opening the show for us. To my surprise, Charles Brown, the singer/pianist who heavily influenced West Coast blues in the 1940s and '50s, came to the club one night to see his old friend Muddy. It was a thrill to meet Musselwhite and only more of one to actually get to play with Brown when Muddy asked him to sit in with us. Yes, he played "Drifting Blues," the song he recorded on the Philo label in 1945, and "Merry Christmas Baby," the classic he recorded for Exclusive two years later.

After the show, I was talking with Muddy and he told me a story about Musselwhite. He said Charlie was the second white person that he remembered seeing in the clubs on the South Side of Chicago in the late 1950s, early '60s. In those days it was still uncommon for young white guys to make their way into the clubs because the South Side could be very dangerous for whites to roam around in, especially young men.

The first one Muddy remembered noticing in the South Side clubs, even before Charlie Musselwhite, was Nick Gravenites, the singer/songwriter. According to Muddy, nobody ever bothered Nick because they thought he was packing. Whether he actually had a gun I don't know, but according to Muddy, nobody messed with Nick.

The way Musselwhite stayed out of trouble was to sit at the bar and not talk to anyone, Muddy told me. "Nobody messed with Charlie because"—Muddy would tap his fingers against his skull to make the point—"everybody thought he was crazy." Years later Charlie and

Handbill, Old Waldorf, San Francisco.

I were playing a festival in Davenport, Iowa, and I told him what Muddy had said. Charlie offered a slight correction. He didn't nurse his drink at the bar in stony silence. There was a waitress that he liked to talk to, he said. I guess Muddy missed that. Charlie laughed at the story and asked me if he could include it in his memoir, if he ever wrote one. Of course, I said, you absolutely can. But I don't think the book has come out.

Chapter 8

GUITAR JUNIOR RETURNS

By then, I had been on the road with Muddy for a few months, still filling in for Guitar Junior. We were in Los Angeles, about to play the Roxy Theatre in early May 1978 when Muddy's manager, Scott Cameron, called me into the dressing room with Muddy. They told me Junior would be ready to rejoin the band in a few weeks, as the tour wound down. I told them that I had known all along that this was going to be temporary work for me, and I thanked Muddy for letting me fill in. But Scott had something more to say. He and Muddy wanted me to stay on as road manager. I didn't say yes on the spot. I was concerned that I might not be doing any guitar playing in this new role. Muddy assured me that he'd have me sit in occasionally. I said I still needed to sleep on it.

The show was about to start so I went to tune my guitar and get ready to go on. Fuzz Jones was seated across from me in the dressing room, doing the same thing. After we were tuned, just to warm up a bit, Fuzz and I started playing "All Your Love," the song Magic Sam recorded (Cobra 5013). And as we were playing, who should walk into the room to say hello to Muddy but Magic Sam's uncle, "Shakey Jake" Harris, the harmonica player. Jake looked at me and said that I sounded like his nephew Sam. Then he walked right over to Muddy and told him he needed a guitar player, and wanted me to stay in LA to play with him. I heard Muddy tell Jake to lay off because I was his boy. I made my way over to where they were talking and asked if I could say something, to which Muddy replied, "You shut up." That gave me something else to sleep on. Do I take a chance with

Jake and stay in LA? Or do I stay on with Muddy and accept his moments-ago offer to be his road manager? It didn't take me long to figure it out. There was no place I would rather be than on the road with Muddy Waters. And that's exactly what I told him first thing the next morning.

Muddy liked Guitar Junior a lot—that's Luther "Guitar Junior" Johnson, not to be confused with Lonnie "Guitar Jr." Brooks or Luther "Snake" Johnson, a member of Muddy's band in the 1960s. One time he said to me, "You know Junior doesn't really play my style, he plays the West Side style real good. And he can holler, he can sing his ass off." What he especially liked, he said, was the way Junior could stir up a crowd. Also that Junior gave Muddy a great introduction as he came on stage. And when they sang something together, Junior could always hold his own. Muddy loved that.

Quite often, if the crowd was clamoring for a second encore and Muddy was tired, he'd send Junior out there. "Go get 'em, Junior." And, lucky me, many times I got to go out and do that encore with Junior, even if I wasn't playing that night. Bob Margolin was really great about it. He would hand me his guitar and tell me to take his place in the band. That really solidified me and Junior—a partnership that would eventually lead to our playing together after Muddy's band fell apart.

Muddy used to say to me privately that, of all the guys in his band, he thought Junior was the one who could really make it on his own. "He's a natural born showman." I heard Muddy say that numerous times. The fact is, all the guys in the band stayed in the business and had successful careers after Muddy.

But, for all his flair and talent, while Junior was with Muddy he had to kind of restrain himself. He could sing, dance, and play—a triple threat. He was in a sideman's role, that was his job; but every once in a while, he'd get a little carried away. He got away with a lot of it because, after all, he was stirring up the crowd for Muddy. But Junior had what it took to sometimes make the crowd his own. If there were people on his side of the stage, he would play to them and they would go crazy. I saw this big time at Milwaukee's Summerfest, in late June.

One of Junior's routines was to lie down on his back and kick his legs up in the air while he was playing a solo. It kind of resembled a cockroach flipped onto its back after a dose of Raid. I saw Junior do this many times when he fronted his own band but never with Muddy's. What he did in Milwaukee was a version of it sort of in reverse. This was an outdoor festival, and there was a railing around the side of the stage where Junior was standing.

Usually the rule was when Muddy gave you a solo, you did twenty-four bars. You took it around twice. If it was really hot he might (very rarely) let you take it a third time. I didn't see too many people get the go-ahead to do three turns. But on this occasion, either the spirit moved Junior, or maybe it was the spirits. I'm not sure which. Whatever his motive, Junior took the solo around twice, like he was supposed to, and then just kept going. A crowd had formed on his side of stage. They were screaming for him and he kept feeding into that and they kept feeding it right back. It became obvious that Junior had taken over, not only the crowd gathered at his side of the stage, but the entire audience. I noticed Muddy looking at Junior trying to get him to end his solo so he could get back into the song. That's when Junior decided to kick it up a notch and hang his belly over the railing. He turned himself into a human seesaw balancing on the rail with his guitar dangling in front of him and his feet kicking in the air behind him. The crowd is roaring and Junior just keeps on playing. I glanced over at Muddy, wondering what the hell he was going to do. How was he going to get Junior to wind it down? At the same time I'm also wondering if Junior is going to fall off the rail and into the crowd below the stage.

Junior was stealing the show. I guess Muddy didn't want to get involved, but he kind of had no choice. He couldn't really stop Junior; the crowd wouldn't have stood for it, so he was going to have to let him play it out. Muddy may have figured Junior wasn't going to be able to keep it up for too long, but he was wrong.

This must have gone on for five minutes, making it the longest solo I saw anybody take with Muddy, ever. But finally, Junior started to lose steam and Muddy ended the song. When Junior came off the stage, I had to wonder what Muddy was going to say. Back in the dressing room, after a few minutes of silence he looked at me and kind of shook his head and started smiling and chuckling to himself. His only comment: "Well, that's Guitar Junior!"

Occasionally, Muddy would ask me to do some spying for him. It was a situation I was reluctant to get into, and I wasn't too good at it. Once in a while, Muddy would do some spying himself. One time on tour, I was getting hungry, so I called Muddy's room and asked if he was going to have dinner. He said, "Yeah, let's have dinner. Meet me down in the restaurant." I spotted Muddy at a table by the entrance, not the booth he usually preferred. I made my way over to the table and started to apologize for being a few minutes late. He told me to be quiet and sit down.

Then he pointed to a nearby table and told me to take a look. Sure enough, there was Guitar Junior, evidently unaware he was under observation. Muddy told me to be quiet so he could hear what Junior was saying. Just then, I noticed an empty booth and asked Muddy if he wanted to move. Nope. Again he hushed me up and kept watching Junior.

Junior was trying to impress his waitress, and Muddy was trying very hard to zero in on Junior's technique as he sweet-talked and clowned for her. He was pulling out all the stops, even serenading this woman of interest. At one point, he reached out to hold her hand. Muddy, clearly entertained by his sideman's floor show, was quietly cheering Junior on: "Go, Junior, go!"

I watched Muddy watching Junior. I watched Junior wooing the waitress. He still had no idea we were sitting right behind him. I couldn't contain myself and started cracking up. Junior glanced over his shoulder and saw me and Muddy. Muddy kept cheering and ratcheted up the volume just a little: "Go, Junior, go!" Junior realized he'd been busted and started laughing. Muddy turned to me with a smile and said, "That Guitar Junior is a natural-born showman. That's why I have him in my band."

As for the waitress, we never did find whether Junior won her over. But it was quite a performance. No doubt about it.

Chapter 9

BREAK IT TO HIM GENTLY

I began my duties as road manager in June 1978 and right away my relationship with Muddy changed. I was a lot more involved in day-to-day decisions on the road, and I became the contact person in his dealings with local media, promoters, and club owners. That made for a lot of conversations with him throughout the day, passing on information I had received or asking him to decide how he wanted me to handle this or that. I also became the banker, so to speak, because it fell to me to collect the money at the end of every gig. Back at the hotel I'd go to Muddy's room and count the take with him.

There was a bit of a learning curve. The first time I started counting money with Muddy, he stopped me cold: "No," he said. "I like mine going the same way." I had no idea of what he was talking about and told him so. What bothered him was that the bills faced every which way, either side up, just as they had when the promoter or club owner gave me the wad. Muddy's view was that if the bills were all going the same way, they were easier to count. So from that night on, I always brought the money to Muddy with all the bills "going the same way." Sometimes at the end of the night when I collected the money from the venue, folks in charge would get annoyed with me because I made sure all the bills were facing in the same direction before I counted them. And then I would count them three times just to make sure the payout was all there. I'm happy to report that I never messed up the money. Not once. I never missed a dollar. Anytime I handed the money to Muddy, it was all there and the bills were in the same direction. The last thing I ever wanted to do was mess up Muddy's money.

I knew that would have riled him, and I definitely didn't want to be on the receiving end of a tirade.

The upside of sitting up late to count money with Muddy was that we would talk. I got one-on-one time with him. He'd be tired, but relaxed and chatty—most of the time. Other times he'd be pissed off about something, and I'd have to listen to him vent. It might be about somebody in the band, or he'd be pissed off at a club owner or promoter for not honoring a percentage in the contract that Muddy felt he was entitled to. Typically, there would be a guaranteed amount versus (usually) 60 percent of gross door receipts, whichever was greater. When I first started collecting the money for Muddy, a club date would usually pay between $2,000 to $2,250 a night. Sometimes there would be one for $2,500. But we came to the unfortunate conclusion that without someone to count heads coming through the door, it was impossible to know (and prove) exactly how many tickets had been sold. Muddy knew he was at the mercy of the club owner to be honest and pay any additional percentage money that was due to him. There were nights when it was obvious the venue was fully packed, I would call this to the club's attention, and they would come up with some bogus numbers for me to look at. Not once during the entire time I worked for Muddy did a club owner pay him a percentage.

Eventually, during these private moments with Muddy I figured out how to tell when something was bothering him. There would be warning signs. One thing I noticed was that when he got a little nervous, especially when money was involved, he would twiddle his thumbs. If he thought he was being ripped off or shorted, things like that, the thumb twiddling would start. That's when I knew to be careful about how much information I let out. I needed to stop short of getting him truly pissed off. He would listen to what I had to say. He might not agree with it, but he would listen. The thumb twiddling was his way of telling me, without his quite realizing it, that I'd better tread lightly and weigh my words. Yes, these conversations could be challenging.

I learned that these one-on-one money-counting sessions were also a good time for me to talk to Muddy about anything that needed to be addressed, including my own concerns. Sometimes our talks would be strictly business. But he could be fatherly if what I needed to talk about was something personal, like dealing with a member of the band who was messing with me. Or dealing with women.

For several months I had been seeing a woman whenever we were in Chicago. If the logistics worked out, she would accompany me to Muddy's shows. Muddy knew her as someone I was dating, someone I was fond of.

I was in Chicago for a night, waiting for the start of our next road trip, when I called and asked her to join me for dinner and drinks. She told me she wasn't feeling well and was going to stay home and rest. I told her I understood and would call her the next day to see how she was doing.

The night was still young so I thought I would grab a bite to eat then go up to the North Side and hear some music. My plan was to make my usual stops—the Wise Fools pub, Kingston Mines, and B.L.U.E.S.—then head back to the hotel. Everything was fine until I made my last stop at B.L.U.E.S., a club I liked to hang out in. It was crowded that night, as usual. I said hello to a few people I knew—and then I spotted her, the woman I had been dating who was not feeling well enough to go out. She was sitting at a table with another man, looking straight at me. I knew the dude and was deeply hurt. She had planned this all along and her claim to be under the weather had been complete bullshit. She didn't have to do what she did to get rid of me. I didn't say a word. I just headed for the door and went back to the hotel to lick my wounds.

The next night I was sitting in the dressing room with Muddy before the gig when he picked up on my misery. "What's wrong with you?" he asked. I told him about being done wrong the night before. He offered up his assessment of the situation: It's kind of like when you're waiting for a bus—I'm not sure Muddy ever waited for a bus—and you get to the bus stop just as one is pulling away. But if you hang around for a little while another one will come along. In his way he was trying to tell me it was going to be all right, that I would find another girl. Somehow it made me feel a lot better.

The best times, as far as I was concerned, were when Muddy was in a great mood with no issues to deal with, women or otherwise. Then it was like hanging out with a friend—much better than being with him in the dressing room with other people hanging around.

I grew to really treasure these conversations. Of course, all the other guys in the band had their own relationships with Muddy. Mine was a little different because I was dealing with money, the management (Scott Cameron), and the promoters. Plus, any information that was coming out of the band would sometimes go to me first, or Muddy would have information he wanted me to pass on to the band. So this was a time when a lot of that would happen.

One thing I learned in these late-night talks was that whatever I wanted to convey to Muddy, I had to do it step by step. I had to learn how to speak to him in a way that wouldn't get him upset. If there was an issue that needed to be addressed, I had to break it to him slowly. For example, if a tire on one of the Suburbans started to look kind of worn, I wouldn't come right out and say, hey, you need new tires on that vehicle. I learned that it kind of had to be his idea, it had to come from him.

By that I mean Muddy didn't like being told what to do. He would listen to what you had to say, but wouldn't necessarily act on it. So, I might say to him, I saw one of the tires was a little low today and when I went to put some air in it, I noticed it was pretty worn out. This was a long way around the block, but I was letting Muddy know that we needed some new tires. I wouldn't say anything else about it. I would just put that out there so he could hear it and mull it over.

The next day, he might go down and check it out himself. Muddy took great care of his vehicles. He always wanted to keep them in top shape because he didn't want us breaking down on the road. After checking out the situation, a day or two later he might say something like: "You know, I was thinking those tires got quite a few miles on them. You better have them checked out, it might be time for some new ones." In other words, it really needed to come from him. Muddy very much wanted to be at the helm. But if you put an idea out there, he would listen. He would think about it, and if it made sense to him, he would go from there. It took some time for me to figure this out.

One topic came up that was particularly delicate. In the years I was around him, Muddy's drink of choice was champagne, Piper-Heidsieck Vintage to be exact. He told me he also used to drink Johnny Walker and Chivas Regal. At some point (I believe it was the early seventies) he dropped the hard stuff. He had also been a heavy smoker, but with health issues beginning to unfold, he gave that up as well. He kept a personal stash of Piper-Heidsieck in a cooler in the basement of his house outside Chicago, so it would always be ready when he was. He loved to sit in the kitchen sipping from the bottle by his side. If I happened to be there, he might open a second bottle and give me a taste.

Muddy was a lot of fun when he drank champagne. It put him in a really good mood. On the road, there was a rider in his contract that specified a bottle of Piper-Heidsieck Vintage for Muddy, and a bottle of Hennessy Cognac that he shared with the band. He would get really upset upon arrival in the dressing room if they didn't have his Piper-Heidsieck or something comparable, like Mumm's or Krug. Once in a while, when a venue couldn't get Piper they would substitute Dom Perignon—better yet! Muddy would be delighted. But if club owners or promoters tried to pass off something that wasn't champagne, Muddy would get furious.

The cognac—Hennessy VSOP (or VS)—was selected with Pinetop in mind. (Pinetop called it Hay-ken-en-essy, for some reason.) But most of the guys would take a little snort, including Muddy, usually just before he stepped out onto the bandstand. In time I noticed him go from real happy to real evil after his snort of cognac. Muddy never got evil when he smoked weed, but the cognac was a problem. The band noticed it, too, and called it to my attention. It got to be a regular thing: the occasional cussing out of a band member after a song ("Motherfucker!"), accompanied by looks that could kill. Jerry Portnoy and Willie Smith came in for the brunt of it, but everyone was getting shellacked.

The guys in the band thought it was best that I talk to Muddy—thanks a lot!—since I was kind of his right-hand man on the road and spent all that time with him each night dealing with the money. I was sitting with him in his room after a show when I summoned my courage and came out with it, choosing my words carefully, as I had learned to do. I told him that when he drank champagne he was always in a great mood. But when he drank cognac on top of that, something happened. He got evil. In total disbelief, Muddy asked me what I was talking about. I told him some of the guys had been noticing it and that I had, too. He told me that I was full of it. I wasn't getting anywhere with him, not right then, but at least I had let the cat out of the bag.

The next night, the same thing happened. He drank the cognac after the champagne. Once again, he quickly went from a great mood to a nasty mood. He was cussing people out, right there on the bandstand. I brought it up again after the show, and it still didn't sink in.

He said he didn't believe me and he didn't want to hear it anymore. I came up with a strategy. I asked him to do something for me: Just for one night, sip your champagne but skip the cognac. "If it doesn't work, then I'm wrong and we're all wrong and you can go back and drink your cognac, or whatever." He mumbled something back at me. "Motherfucker" was in there along with some other choice words. But to my surprise he actually agreed to try it for one night. The next show he drank champagne, no cognac, and everything went fine. He still wasn't convinced.

After the show I pointed out that he hadn't got evil. He didn't get pissed off at anybody and he had a good time. Everybody had a good time. The word "shit" was among the words he grumbled to me, and right away he went back to drinking cognac with his Piper-Heidsieck and getting evil on stage. The situation was turning really unpleasant.

This was an example of how you could sometimes talk to Muddy in a very direct way, but other times you were better off planting an idea in his head and letting him mull it over in his own good time and then come to think of it as his own. That was fine with me. Sometimes Pinetop Perkins would say something. Maybe that's what finally convinced Muddy.

Whatever got him to this point, one night Muddy mentioned that maybe he needed to cut out the Hennessy and just stick with champagne. And, by god, that's what he did. It didn't calm all the tensions onstage, but it sure did help.

Of course, with some issues it was best not to get Muddy involved at all.

Chapter 10

CONTROL FREAK

There was a very good friend of mine who was also friends with Muddy—Joe Berson. Muddy mentions him, but not by name, in a song he wrote called "Deep Down in Florida" and included on *Hard Again*, the 1977 album he did for Blue Sky. In the second verse Muddy sings, "Well, I think I'll go down to Gainesville just to see an old friend of mine." That's Joe Berson. Joe was a really great harmonica player. He was originally from Brooklyn but had moved to Florida in the mid-seventies to go to school in Gainesville, which is where Muddy met him. Muddy also met Marva Jean Brooks down there, the future wife that he called "Sunshine." She was from a little Florida town called Newberry.

Joe had relocated to Chicago not long before I started working with Muddy, and besides being a talented musician he was quite a character. When I arrived in Chicago, he was living in a dive on Ohio Street called the Tokyo Hotel. Dan Aykroyd and John Belushi became friends with Joe after seeing him play with guitarist and vocalist Jimmy Rogers, Muddy's partner in the late 1940s and early '50s. There's a scene in their *Blues Brothers* movie—a cheap hotel room with Chicago's el train rattling by the window—that I'm fairly sure was inspired by Joe's digs at the Tokyo. It sums up the life he was living at that time because of his devotion to playing the blues. When we were in Chicago, I would frequently stay with other members of Muddy's band at a hotel down the street from the Tokyo. One night Joe met me to hitch a ride with the band to Muddy's gig at a venue outside Chicago called Harry Hopes, a drive of about an hour. Our two-night engagement in late August was going to be recorded for Muddy's next album, *Muddy Mississippi Waters Live*.

Johnny Winter, the Texas-born blues rock legend, was to play and produce the record, and Columbia/Blue Sky sent out a truck from the Record Plant in New York to tape the show. Winter's manager at that time was a wired, controlling kind of guy named Teddy Slatus. He watched over Winter like a hawk, and it seemed to me that Johnny was always testing the waters with Teddy. When Johnny was getting ready to do a guest appearance with Muddy and the band, I would see Teddy pacing around the dressing room with a clipboard in his hand. His usual routine was yelling at people, kicking people out of the dressing room (including me), and creating a bad vibe in general. I viewed him as a total control freak.

One night during the Harry Hopes sessions, I walked into the dressing room to alert Johnny that Muddy was about to call him out onto the stage. True to form, Slatus immediately tried to kick me out. I'm sorry but I work for Muddy, I told him, and I need to be in here for a minute. Teddy goes ballistic: "Get out! You have to get out of here!" That kind of thing. Well, I was in no mood for his bullshit, so I stood my ground and told him I wasn't going to leave.

Johnny liked to tune up with a harmonica, but didn't have one handy. Back then, in the late seventies, the little portable guitar tuners were not yet common. Few guitar players had them. For lack of a harmonica, Johnny started freaking out, telling Slatus that if he can't tune his guitar with a harmonica, he's not going out on stage. Fortunately, Joe Berson, who was with me that night to see the show, always had a harp on him, a Hohner Marine Band. I made my way over to where he was seated in the audience, explained the situation, and asked if Johnny could borrow it. Joe was reluctant. He said he didn't want anyone playing his harp. Somehow, I talked him into letting Johnny use it. We made our way back to the dressing room to break the good news that I had found someone who had a harmonica for Johnny to tune up with. Johnny immediately tried to grab the goods from Joe, who had just hit an E note on his Hohner so Johnny could tune up. That wasn't good enough; Johnny wanted to play the note himself.

Meanwhile, Slatus was raging at us to leave. I remember saying to him, "Look, if you want this to happen, you're going to have to let us stay in here, because Johnny wants this harmonica, and if Joe leaves he's taking it with him." From my experience, Johnny was an easygoing guy to just sit and talk to one-on-one. But with Slatus around, pushing everybody's buttons, Johnny would go off on him. It was like there was a power struggle between the two of them.

So, Teddy wanted to kick us out, Johnny needed to get a harmonica, the tape was rolling recording the show live, and Muddy was getting ready to call Johnny to the stage. This was now a perfect storm. Finally, Joe gave Winter his harmonica, Johnny tuned up, and thanked Joe for letting him use it. Then, as Johnny gets up to join Muddy on stage, he inadvertently slips the harmonica into his pocket. Joe says: "Johnny, can I have my harmonica back? You've got my harp. Give me my harp."

I could only pray that this wouldn't escalate into another shouting match, because Joe was another guy with a very short fuse. Fortunately, Johnny gave him his harp and the harmonica fiasco was over.

That mess was a close call, but not all that unusual. Anytime Slatus was around, I knew I had to fasten my seatbelt because chaos might ensue. Muddy loved Johnny like a son and was deeply indebted to him. When Muddy's contract with Chess Records expired in 1975, Johnny had helped get the deal with Columbia/Blue Sky. Muddy had great respect for Johnny as a player, too. "Johnny can play a hundred notes to my one, but when I play that one, I make it count," Muddy said one time.

The problem was that when Johnny came to pay his respects, Teddy would usually be with him, and I had to be careful not to get into any of his nonsense. I found it hard to respect him, but I had to be wary of the way he could sabotage the whole show. All that foolishness over Joe's harmonica and Teddy yelling at us to get out was nothing more than an effort to get Johnny Winter to hit the stage on cue. No one in the audience knew what went on in the dressing room that night, nor did Muddy.

Chapter 11

LOVE IN A MODEL T

Muddy was an old-timer—the oldest or second-oldest guy in the band, depending on whether you believed his passport or the rumors that said he was born earlier than he claimed. Either way, he was full of lore about the way things used to be, and he liked to share it. Life on the road gave him an opportunity. We passed downtime in the hotels visiting with each other, playing cards, watching TV, or just bullshitting. Willie and Pinetop always shared a room and welcomed visitors, so you could always drop by unannounced. I loved spending time with both of them.

Before a show Muddy and Pinetop would often pass the time playing a card game I couldn't figure out (even though Muddy tried to teach it to me). I think it might have been called casino. They'd be sitting there slamming cards down on the table in friendly competition. But somewhere along the way, usually in the middle of the game, it seemed like they always got into an argument about who was older. Muddy would just bust Pinetop: "You know you're a lot older than I am, man." Pinetop would return fire: "Mud, you know that's not true because they done messed up your birth certificate so you just as old as me, you might even be older." I heard this routine play out on more than a few occasions.

As far as I knew, Muddy was born in 1915. When we went through customs together, or anytime I had to deal with Muddy's passport or immigration form, his birthday was listed as April 4, 1915. But then, a few years ago, someone discovered that Muddy was actually born in 1913, the same year as Pinetop. So, somewhere along the way 1913 turned into 1915. Why and when this happened I will never know.

Muddy's immigration form for Vancouver, BC dates (February 8–9, 1980).

Hmm, apparently Pinetop was onto something.

One time I knocked on the door. Willie Smith opened it and I walked in. Unexpectedly, Muddy was in there and so was most of the band. The guys stood around while Muddy demonstrated something in great detail. He had everyone's attention, so I figured I better pay attention too. Whatever Muddy was talking about, he went step by step, getting more and more animated as he went along. Now he was on Willie's bed, demonstrating how you put your left leg up here and your right leg over there, because this or that would be in the way. Then he said something about a running board—running board?—and started humping away on the bed. "That's how you do it," he said, getting up off the bed. I'm still in the dark. "Do what?" I asked him. "What the hell are you doing?" His answer was blunt, and also unexpected: "I'm trying to teach these boys how to fuck in a Model T Ford."

So, here we were, it's the late 1970s, a half century since the last Model T rolled off the assembly line, and Muddy is giving a tutorial on how to do the wild thing in one of them.

Later on I heard other guys tell this tale, Bob Margolin among them, so I know I didn't make it up.

Somewhere in my busy first year with Muddy, he took us to New Orleans, where I played on one of my all-time favorite gigs, the 1978 New Orleans Jazz & Heritage Festival (known as Jazz Fest). On April 14, we played on the riverboat SS *Admiral* with B.B. King and Roosevelt Sykes. Playing on the riverboat was pure magic. It was a thrill for me to hear (and meet) Roosevelt Sykes, a New Orleans–based singer and piano player. Backstage, I told him I had seen a decades-old picture of him in a car with Victoria "Queen Victoria" Spivey, a blues singer/songwriter and piano player whose career spanned forty years (1926–76). It had been my privilege to meet Spivey and perform with her, I told Roosevelt. He smiled and told me he remembered the picture being taken. Maybe he had a great memory or was just being polite, I didn't know. But I was happy to meet him.

Now it was time for Muddy's show to begin, so I made my way to the stage. The boat was still docked at the foot of Canal Street as Muddy made his entrance, but as soon as he settled onto his stool the boat started moving. Startled, Muddy looked to his left where Jerry Portnoy and I were standing and said "Shiiiiit, we rolling." We didn't know the Admiral would be cruising on the river for Muddy's and B.B. King's shows. What a wonderful time we had; Muddy clearly enjoyed himself being with his good friend B.B.

New Orleans Jazz Fest performance, riverboat SS Admiral (April 14, 1978). Photo by D. Shigley.

The next night we had a club date at the Kingfish in Baton Rouge. Muddy surprised everyone that night by cuing "Louisiana Blues," a song he rarely played. There's a part in the song where Muddy sings, "I'm going down in New Orleans and get me a mojo hand" and on the original record Little Walter chimed in with, "Take me witcha, man, when you go." Muddy was in a playful mood that night when he turned his head and looked back at the band as he sang Little Walter's response. We all cracked up, Muddy was always dead serious when he sang; for him to add Little Walter's ad lib was totally out of character. It was great when Muddy would show his sense of humor.

The next day we played Jazz Fest again, only this time it was at the Fairgrounds, a racetrack that has traditionally served as the festival's main venue. It had rained earlier that day and the track was a muddy mess. We arrived at the wrong entrance gate and had no idea of where our stage was located. Muddy didn't like to be kept waiting, so he decided one of us should get out of the vehicle and see which of the ten stages we'd be playing. Since I was the new kid on the block, he decided I should be the one to get out and find it. Along with the mud underfoot, it was hot as hell that day and I wanted to get the search over with fast. While Muddy and the rest of the band waited in the air-conditioned Suburbans, I ran around frantically until I found our stage, which—of course—turned out to be at the far end of the racetrack. I was in a foul mood as I met the stage manager who would handle our set, a guy named Phil Tripp. Phil was under pressures of his own. We were already running late, he said, and I needed to get my butt back to where the band was parked and bring them to the stage ASAP. So off I ran, retracing my steps.

As music extravaganzas go, New Orleans's mid-spring blowout remains one of the best. Muddy loved playing Jazz Fest, and the crowd response was as warm as the weather. The Fest was run by Quint Davis, in those days still in collaboration with the late George Wein, the founder of Newport's jazz and folk festivals. We came to appreciate that anything staged by Festival Productions, as their company was called, would be top-notch. After working several shows together, Phil and I became friends, and Muddy, a connoisseur of folks he described as "characters," soon realized that Phil was a classic case. He enjoyed having him around. It didn't hurt that Phil was very respectful of Muddy and gracious in his dealings with us.

An upside to working for Muddy was that you never knew who might show up at a gig. One example: A couple of months after Jazz Fest, on July 8 the Rolling Stones played Soldier Field in Chicago before an audience of about 80,000. That night rumor had it that, along with Willie Dixon, they would be coming to see Muddy at a small Chicago club called the Quiet Knight—capacity: a few hundred. Word had spread and when I arrived at the club that evening there was already a line from the entrance well down West Belmont Avenue. It would only grow as showtime approached. Keep an eye out and bring Willie and the Stones to the dressing room, Muddy instructed me.

The Stones were still huge in '78 and it's worth remembering their links to Muddy's world. Not only had the Stones borrowed the name of their band from Muddy's 1950 song, "Rollin' Stone," but, along with other luminaries of sixties British rock—Eric Clapton comes to mind—they had promoted the Delta and Chicago blues sound, and invited some of the original perpetrators of that sound to open for them on world tours, Muddy included.

I was going about my usual preshow duties as road manager when a sudden buzz in the audience told me the Stones had arrived. I made my way to the dressing room and found Muddy with an arm wrapped around his buddy Keith Richards, the Stones' guitarist and secondary vocalist. Muddy introduced me to Keith, then gave me two orders: "Get more champagne, and when Mick arrives bring him to me." This was Muddy's party, and he wanted the bubbly to be flowing. I went looking for the club owner, the late Richard Harding, to get more champagne. Harding took me into the stock room and provided me with a couple of bottles. As soon as I handed them to Muddy, he told me to go get more. I stepped out of the dressing room, and there was Mick Jagger, standing in the hallway alone. I told him I worked for Muddy and that he had asked me to bring him back to the dressing room. "Yes. Muddy. Please take me to him," Mick said in his courtly British way.

That still left part two of Muddy's request: more champagne! I found the club owner again, but this time Harding was not so quick to hand over more bottles. He reminded me how much Muddy had already gone through that evening—to which I replied: How often do you have Muddy Waters and the Rolling Stones in your club on the same night? Harding answered by opening another case and handing over a few more bottles. I made my way back into the dressing room, opened the champagne and, at Muddy's behest, went around the room topping off glasses.

When I asked Ron Wood if he would like some champagne, he said yes and grabbed the nearly full bottle. I told him I was thinking more like a glass. (Oh, well, I thought to myself, it's only rock and roll.) There were many more people than chairs in the dressing room, so after handing Ron the bottle I offered a guitar road case for him to sit on, which he did. Since I had no place to sit, he offered to share it with me. I found him to be a nice, easygoing guy. Of course the highlight of the evening was when Muddy called the Stones to join him onstage for a few songs, including "Got My Mojo Working" with Muddy and Mick trading off vocals. Muddy really loved the Stones and how they helped bring his music to a world audience. He never lost sight of that.

Rolling Stones and Muddy (Quiet Knight, Chicago, July 1978).
Photo by D. Shigley. Abaca Press/Alamy Stock Photo.

In early August, we were at ChicagoFest when Scott Cameron told us that President Jimmy Carter had invited Muddy to perform later that week at the annual White House staff picnic. We were already booked to do three nights at a Washington club called the Cellar Door, so this was going to mesh well with our plans. The first night was a surprise, Fleetwood Mac showed up at the club to see Muddy. Since Muddy, in typical fashion, didn't know their names, he called them up to sit in by bellowing, "Fleetwood Mac . . . Fleetwood Mac"—and only the drummer, Mick Fleetwood, responded. I later learned from a waitress that when she went to their table to take drink orders, they only wanted "a mirror"—presumably to enjoy stimulants other than alcohol.

The last date in DC would be a doubleheader, the White House in the daytime and the Cellar Door that night. The only other detail that Scott had for us was that there would be no pay for the performance for the president. Upon hearing that, Guitar Junior informed Muddy that he would not be able to make the trip to Washington because he had some family business to tend to. Muddy didn't question him but instead turned to me. "Okay, you play," he said. This would not be the

The White House lawn (August 1978).

first time I covered for Junior; after all, that's how I started working for Muddy in the first place—filling in while Junior recovered from his fall in Boston.

I was honored to do the gig, pay or no pay. The icing on the cake for me was that I also got to meet the president and First Lady Rosalynn Carter. Muddy was deeply moved by the invitation to play the White House: "Ain't no president ever invited me to his house before." To my surprise, a few months after the gig a photo of us on the bandstand arrived in the mail for me. It was signed "Best wishes Jimmy Carter." I still have it somewhere.

Chapter 12

ELTON WHO?

A few days after the White House gig we were in New York for the Dr. Pepper Summer Music Festival (August 11, 1978) at the Wollman Skating Rink in Central Park. Muddy was opening for Bonnie Raitt. Since I had grown up just outside the city, I had been in the audience for the Pepper Fest more than a few times. That included Bob Margolin's first show with Muddy in 1973. (Michael "Hollywood Fats" Mann was also in the band at the time, on guitar.) But this would be the first time I ever actually worked the festival and, needless to say, I was looking forward to it.

The afternoon before the show, I drove one of the Suburbans over to the Wollman Rink so I could scope out the lay of the land and figure the best route to the stage. Much to my surprise (and enjoyment), the only way to get to the stage was to drive over the curb and across the grass. (Thanks go to the NYPD for instructing me to do just that!). Back at the hotel, I told Muddy what time we would have to leave for the show. Muddy said I should drive the lead vehicle and let the other guys follow in the second Suburban since I knew my way around New York. I was fine with that. I knew the city's rules of the road, cab-driver style. Forget about using your turn signal to change lanes; just give a beep or two on the horn and move on over. I had cabbie in my blood; my grandfather drove a New York taxi for forty years!

I did not inform Muddy of the travel details to Central Park that evening. He trusted that I had it all worked out. My parents were coming to visit me at the hotel and would be riding with us to the gig. Muddy always liked to sit up front in the passenger seat and keep careful watch over whoever was driving. It stemmed from a traffic accident he had had in the late sixties, and it made him a nervous passenger. He would not hesitate to let you know if he thought you were driving too fast, or getting too close to another vehicle. If he saw someone driving kind of crazy, winding in and out of traffic and trying to pass you, he would say, "Let him go ahead on, let him go." He wanted the crazy drivers to be in front of him not behind him so he could see where they were and what they were doing.

So, here we were, getting ready to leave the hotel, and I'm about to break all of Muddy's rules for safe driving. Maybe having my parents in the vehicle helped calm him down a bit, I don't know. Off we went through the streets of Manhattan on our way to Central Park. I was doing all the cab driver moves, and honking the horn as I cut from lane to lane. So far so good. Not a word from Muddy about my driving. But soon the critical moment would arrive.

As we approached Central Park, I told Muddy I had to jump the curb because there was no other way to do this. I was relieved and surprised when he told me that I must know what I'm doing, so go ahead. I jumped the curb and started driving across the grass. The cops were waving me through because of the parking pass on the dashboard. Muddy didn't say a word to me, he just went along for the ride. No problem!

He did the show, and everything was going well. Sitting in the dressing room waiting to hear Bonnie Raitt play, he was in a really good mood. He loved her singing and slide-guitar work. He had a lot of respect for Bonnie. He was also very kind to my parents as they watched the goings on backstage and in the dressing room. He was generous enough to share his champagne with them, something they appreciated. While we relaxed, various people came for a visit. One of them was Elton John. Someone in his entourage knocked on the door and yelled out: "Elton John to see Muddy, Elton John to see Muddy." Muddy drew a blank: "Elton who? Elton John? I don't know no Elton John, get him out of here."

So that was that. Elton John had been there to see Bonnie but wanted to pay his respects to Muddy—who didn't have a clue who he was. This sometimes happened: a run-in with a big star that Muddy didn't know, no matter how famous they might be. He meant no offense. Elton John and Muddy meeting each other just wasn't in the cards—at least not right then. We would have another encounter with Elton John, but that was four months ahead.

Starting on September 21, we had a four-day dream gig: A festival in Hawaii, the Kool Pacific Music Fair to be held at the Waikiki Shell in Honolulu. This festival would be produced by Festival Productions, the same people who do the New Orleans Jazz and Heritage Festival and many others. Muddy and the band knew we would be in good hands, and we were: oceanfront rooms, a light schedule (six fifty-minute sets over four days). Paradise! What's not to like?

It all ended too soon because our next gig, five days later, would be on the other side of the United States in Monroe, Maine. Not a palm tree in sight. It was back to the grind of life on the road for a hard-traveling band, but all was not bad. We drove from Chicago to Maine and the farther east we went, the more beautiful the fall foliage got. In a matter of days we had glimpsed two extremes, both equally charming in their own ways, I thought.

PART
TWO

Chapter 13

A BIG BRIT

We were finishing some dates in Canada in November 1978 when Muddy called everyone into the dressing room to make an announcement. We were leaving for Europe almost immediately to begin a tour with a big British rock star. And who might this rock star be? Bob Margolin and I started quizzing Muddy. The only thing he knew was that he was a guitar player. So we named names. Jimmy Page? Jeff Beck? Eric Clapton? The first two didn't ring a bell, but when Muddy heard Clapton's name he said that's the one. Fresh back from Canada, we all went home to pack for a five-week tour of Europe, opening for Eric Clapton.

Blue Sky Records, the record company that had Muddy under contract, which was distributed by Columbia Records (by CBS in Britain), was to provide advertising and some financial support for the tour. They were excited about it. Opening for Clapton was an opportunity for Muddy to reach a larger audience, possibly a whole new generation of record buyers. And Blue Sky's distributor offered financial support to help the band and me with daily expenses for five weeks in Europe.

I got to play some dates on the tour, but mostly I wore my road-manager hat. We hit our first snag shortly after arriving in France.

Our first stop was Lyon. After checking into the hotel, I met with Muddy in his room. He handed me the per diem money for the band in the form of checks to help with their expenses. I was told they were to be distributed to every band member a week at a time. I noticed they were drawn on Muddy's bank, the Bank of Westmont. As in Westmont, Illinois, a town not on the tip of every tongue here in France. Scott Cameron, Muddy's manager, figured the band and I would be able to cash them anywhere in Europe. Guess again, Scott. As I quickly learned after some of the guys tried to cash their first check, there wasn't a bank anywhere around that would touch them.

I reported the problem to Muddy: no money for per diem expenses—such as food (and the guys are getting hungry!). Muddy was pissed: "I told Scott the checks wouldn't work." We put our heads together and came up with a plan. I suggested we get the money wired to a bank in Europe and see if we could convert it into American Express Travelers Cheques. Muddy said it was worth a try, so we called Cameron's office back in the States. Success. He arranged to have the funds wired to a bank in Germany, one of the next stops on the tour. The plan was for Muddy and I to go to the bank, withdraw the money in travelers checks, and distribute them to the guys on a weekly schedule.

Upon arrival, Muddy and I ventured over to the designated German bank and sat down with one of the officers. He produced the books of travelers checks, a total of $7,000, all in twenties. Muddy observed the pile of checks—350 all told. They needed to be signed. His response was predictable and brief. "I'm not gonna sign them, there's too many checks. You sign them." I wanted to be sure that I heard him right. "You want me to sign all these traveler's checks?" His answer: "Yeah, I'll sit here, you sign them." I asked whose name I should use. The banker said it didn't matter. "Use yours," Muddy said. And so I set to work. It seemed like hours, Muddy sitting there grumpily while I scribbled my name 350 times. When it was finally over, I reached for a little briefcase I had with me and put the travelers checks inside. I looked at Muddy: "Oh, boy! Seven thousand dollars. I'm young. I'm in Europe. This could be a pretty good time for me." Muddy looked at me and said, "You shut up. Come on, let's get out of here."

No, I did not take off with the American Express travelers checks. Muddy knew I was joking and laughed about it. But to my workload had been added another responsibility, treasurer. I had become the band's bank, with responsibility to keep track of the $200 a week I distributed to each member.

There was another fly in the ointment. Before the start of the tour, Cameron had instructed me to be sure when we got to the end of the tour, or perhaps every week, that I collect the unspent portion of the per diem money, then return it to him. I was incredulous. "You want me to do what?" He repeated, "It's $200 a week for the guys and whatever money they don't spend you tell them to give it back to you at the end of the tour. Collect all of it and give it to Muddy to bring back to me."

The guys were all happy to get the money, no doubt about that. But when I told them about Scott wanting them to return unspent money, I got basically the same answer from every one of them: "Give him what back? You tell him he can kiss my ass." And every one of them offered a prediction: "There isn't gonna be anything left, I guarantee." I didn't pass along the invitation to kiss ass, but I told Cameron not to count on getting any of the money back, unless he wanted to fly over and ask for it personally. Europe, as it turned out, wasn't in his travel plans just then.

The tour opened on November 8, 1978, at the Palais des Sport in Lyon, and Eric came out into the stage wings to watch Muddy open for him. They passed each other as Muddy was coming off stage, and Eric said hello. I don't think Muddy knew who he was. For the next couple of nights, the same thing happened. Eric would come to the show, sit off to the side of the stage, and watch Muddy. The buzz was that Eric's shows weren't going as well as they could have, while Muddy was in great form. The opening act was overpowering the featured attraction.

By the third night, Eric's manager, Roger Forrester, pulled me aside. "What the hell is going on here?" he demanded. I told him I didn't know what he was talking about. "What's going on with Muddy? What's he doing?" He said they had the same problem when Freddie King toured with them, Freddie always trying to upstage Eric.

I explained to Roger that Muddy wasn't doing anything different. This was a normal show for him. I told him that Muddy was just really "heavy." That's what made Muddy Muddy. "We'll see about that," Forrester snapped. The next night he came out and watched part of

Muddy's show with Eric, then approached me afterwards. "Okay, I see what you mean," he said.

Clapton, I guess, was kind of freaked out to have to follow Muddy's set on these early tour dates. As was widely known, he had great respect for all the older bluesmen. So Forrester came up with a plan. He decided to time Eric's arrival each night with the last minutes of Muddy's set. That way Eric could enjoy just a song or two of Muddy's before going onstage to do his own show. In the program for his US tour the following year, Eric admitted that he could not watch Muddy before going on stage himself. Watching Muddy's show completely drained him. That was pretty strong stuff coming from one of the best guitar players on the planet!

Roger's plan made sense to me. Let Eric have only a few moments listening to Muddy instead of being there for the whole show and losing his nerve. I suggested to Forrester that it also might help if Muddy and Eric spent some time together, get to know each other, get comfortable. I wanted Roger to let Eric know that Muddy was very approachable. It needed to happen ASAP or this was going to be a long and difficult tour. As we were having the conversation, it suddenly dawned on me how to bring it off. With Eric sitting in the wings each night as Muddy finished his set, why not have them chat for a few minutes before Eric stepped onstage to do his own show?

What I had in mind was this: As Muddy ended his set and walked offstage, I usually retrieved the guitar he had left on the bandstand and brought it to his dressing room. How about if I handed it to Eric and asked him to return it to Muddy's room? It might break the ice. So one night as I was coming off the stage with Muddy's guitar, I asked Eric if he could help me with something. He was very gracious. He wanted to know what he could do. I held out Muddy's guitar and asked if he could carry it backstage. Eric kind of stiffened. He said he couldn't do it. It was Muddy's guitar, which made it kind of magic. I could relate to that. It was the same feeling I had about six months earlier when former Allman Brothers' road manager Twiggs Lyndon invited me to play the late Duane Allman's Les Paul. I tried again, telling Eric it would be a real favor, because I had to get something else off the stage. When Eric still seemed reluctant, I told him I'd go back to Muddy's dressing room with him.

Which is what happened. Several years ago I saw a book that mentioned the same moment but got one detail of the story wrong. It stated that Bob Margolin handed Muddy's guitar to Eric Clapton. Nope. It was me.

In the dressing room, Eric asked Muddy where he should put the guitar? Muddy pointed to his guitar case and told him to lay it down there. Then Muddy said something to Eric that I hoped wouldn't ruin the moment. Muddy in his huge voice: "Thanks, Clapton."

Eric turned and looked at Muddy. "You don't even know my name, do you!" I was hoping Muddy was going to say the right thing, otherwise this might get really awkward. Muddy looked at Eric and said, "Sure I know your name." Eric wasn't so sure: "Okay, what's my name?"

Muddy replied in a very slow, drawn-out voice, "Er-r-ric Clap-ton! Eric Clapton!" At that point everyone (especially me) breathed a huge sigh of relief. The ice had been broken. The two of them started talking and within a short time they developed a really great relationship. From time to time, Eric would ask Muddy to come out during his set and play with him. No dice. Muddy informed Eric that he would be happy to sing with him, but not to play guitar. That was Muddy's policy, he would sing with other bands, but not play guitar. Muddy meant no disrespect. He loved the way Eric played. He thought Eric's band was top-notch. But Muddy was more comfortable playing guitar with his own band. They understood his sound and his timing.

Many nights on the tour I would have moments with Muddy while standing on the side of the stage waiting for Eric to call for him to come out. As we waited, Muddy would often comment to me about how much he enjoyed Eric's playing. Especially when he played slide guitar. Muddy would say to anyone within earshot: "Listen to what he's playing, did you hear that?" Muddy could track Clapton's playing to its roots. "Eric got that from Robert Johnson," he said one time. Or, "That sounds like something he got from me."

As the tour went on, a kind of father/son relationship developed. Muddy's admiration for Eric was mixed with a little worry about the boy. This was a period when Eric was drinking a lot. Watching from the side of the stage, Muddy would comment to me how much Eric was sweating. Muddy had seen that before, the way booze wreaks havoc on the body and makes people sweat like crazy. He knew it usually didn't end well. He was fearful of what might happen to Eric if he didn't slow down.

On that first night in Lyon, with the band getting ready to go on, I spotted Bill Wyman, the Rolling Stones bassist, backstage. I think he was living in France at the time and made his way over to the gig to see Muddy. He knew Muddy from way back in the early days of the Rolling Stones. When Muddy was in Europe or the Rolling Stones traveled to the states, their paths would sometimes cross. But Wyman had not made it to the Quiet Knight a few months earlier when the Stones showed up at the Chicago club to see Muddy.

After spotting Wyman, I spoke to the stage manager and asked who was going to introduce Muddy's band. No one. They weren't planning to do that kind of introduction. I went over to Wyman and told him that I worked for Muddy, then asked him if he spoke French, he said he did. I explained the situation and asked him if he would mind introducing Muddy's band because there wasn't anyone to do it. I realized I was putting him on the spot, but he said he'd be delighted. With that, he strode out onto the stage, grabbed the microphone and started speaking in French. I don't speak French, so I'm not sure what he said, but he ended it by introducing the Muddy Waters Blues Band. The crowd erupted, he walked off the stage and over to where I was standing.

I was feeling pretty good about finding someone at the last second to introduce Muddy's band in French—a Rolling Stone, no less! So, I thanked him profusely. I was not prepared for his response. He looked at me and said, "You know, nobody knew who I was." That seemed unlikely to me: "Everybody knows who you are." He seemed kind of upset and said it again: "I don't think anybody knew who I was when I went out there." I tried to reassure him that everyone knows Bill Wyman of the Rolling Stones, and that everybody recognized him, at least the ones close enough to see him.

Andrew Zweck, tour manager, Europe 1978. Photo by Brian Bisesi.

Maybe he was disappointed that the audience didn't scream at the sight of him, or something like that. I don't know. But after the show, Jerry Portnoy came up to me and told me I should have had someone introduce Bill Wyman before I had him introduce the band. It just never dawned on me that people wouldn't know who he was. My mistake. If Bill Wyman ever reads this, I apologize. I should have had someone introduce you. But it all ended well: Muddy was happy to see Bill and I learned something that night about introducing introducers. Thanks again to Bill Wyman for doing that introduction.

We were assigned a tour manager for our five weeks with Clapton. His name was Andy Zweck. Andy was an Australian. He was a great help to us, and I learned a lot from being around him. He was a very experienced tour and road manager. I found him both interesting and amusing. He would always be asking for things from venues and promoters. I would mention something that needed to happen, and right away he was on the phone arranging whatever it was that we needed. After relaying our request, he would always follow with "Can you make it happen?" This cracked me up.

Sometimes the person on the other end of the call could make it happen, and sometimes he couldn't. I asked Andy why he always used that approach. He told me his philosophy: "We're going to ask them for this, and the worst they can tell us is no." He always approached everything that way. It really stuck with me. I found it fascinating to see how many balls he could juggle at one time. When the need was to make something happen, Andy was the wizard, not the guy on the other end of the call. I was very thankful to have him out there with us. It was a real education for me.

Chapter 14

ALL ABOARD! (EXCEPT US)

We traveled through Europe by bus. Eric and his band traveled by train, their own private train. Muddy was uncomfortable on the bus because it was really cold, and so was Pinetop Perkins. Muddy would sit behind the bus driver and ask him repeatedly to turn the heat up—which the guy never really did. As a result, Muddy wound up getting pretty sick at one point. It was kind of a head-scratcher why Eric didn't invite Muddy to ride on the train with him. Muddy would have been a lot more comfortable.

One night, Jerry Portnoy, Bob Margolin, and I were invited onto the train to hang out with Eric. Carl Radle, his bass player, and Jamie Oldaker, the drummer, were there too. We learned it was an historic train. They were filming this tour for a movie, to be called *The Rolling Hotel*. That's what Eric and company called the train: Eric Clapton's Rolling Hotel. They filmed parts of the tour on stage, backstage, and on the train. Although the film was never officially released, I've noticed there are bootleg copies of it floating around.

Radle gave me kind of a history lesson about the car we were sitting in. During World War II it had been at the disposal of Hermann Göring (or Goering), one of the most powerful military and political leaders in Hitler's Nazi party. Radle said we were seated in what had been the conference car, the place where Göring and his generals plotted their war against the Allies. I was fascinated by this, but also chilled. I always enjoyed talking with Carl. He was a bit older than me. Eric's band referred to him as the "old man." By then he was in his midthirties.

Muddy on the bus. Photo by Bob Margolin.

Carl was American, not British, and he had had some interesting incarnations in the course of his career. I had seen him at the Fillmore East in New York when he was with Joe Cocker's Mad Dogs and Englishmen. He told me he really enjoyed the Fillmore show, one of his all-time favorite gigs. From Mad Dogs the conversation segued to his work with Clapton's Derek and the Dominos, a group I had also seen at the Fillmore East. (I was pretty much a regular there as a teenager). He had played and recorded with some of the greats: George Harrison, Rita Coolidge, Leon Russell—you name it. Carl was a really kind person and great bass player. He was very respectful of Muddy and of all the old blues artists. He had played with Freddie King. So I was lucky to spend time with him. He had a long history in music and very unfortunate demise. A mix of drugs and booze took him out. He was all of thirty-seven when he died.

The bus rides sometimes brought Muddy's memories alive. One time he got to reminiscing with me about his first trip across the Atlantic. It was in 1958, for a UK tour with Otis Spann, his piano player. Muddy arrived with a brand-new Fender Telecaster, not realizing that British audiences hadn't quite caught up to the electric style he had been playing in Chicago. Or so Muddy concluded from a review that said something snippy about a "screaming guitar." (Shades of Bob Dylan's reception from folk fans after he went electric at the Newport Festival in 1965.)

In England, Muddy introduced me to a colleague from that era, Chris Barber, the jazz virtuoso. Chris played both trombone and double bass. He went out of his way to be helpful to American acts tackling England for the first time, Muddy included. Chris brought Muddy and Otis to England and provided his band to back them. I wish I had thought to ask him about what British audiences made of Muddy and Otis on that earlier trip. Muddy had great respect for Chris and all he did for American and English musicians.

Because of the frosty reaction to his shift to an electric guitar, the next time Muddy went to England he brought an acoustic instrument—only to find out that they wanted him to play electric. For his third trip, he brought both and would ask the audience which one they wanted to hear. I'm not sure how it all worked out, but that's a story Muddy told me.

Traveling with Muddy—as with any showbiz personality—was always interesting because of how often someone recognized him. It happened in airports, in restaurants. Usually it was a fan who had seen the show somewhere. Occasionally, it would be another celebrity. The question was always whether Muddy would recognize the celebrity who had recognized him—and it made for awkward moments.

In late 1978, Rod Stewart had a huge hit with "Da Ya Think I'm Sexy?" And by early '79 it was all over the radio, in the disco clubs, everywhere, just blasting away.

"What kind of song is that?" Muddy would gripe, if anyone was around.

Muddy thought it was the most ridiculous thing he'd ever heard. I know he appreciated that somebody was making a lot of money off it, and I'm sure he wouldn't have minded if it was him. But he just couldn't wrap his head around that song. Of course, when you really think about it, the song is quite brilliant, a reflection of what was going on in a lot of the clubs at that time. Regardless, Muddy still thought it was silly, and as often as not he'd chime in with his own version of the lyrics: "Do you want my body? Do you want my body? Yes, I want your body."

Before too long, Muddy came up with a little dance to go with it. Muddy's dance kind of reminded me of an episode from the classic 1950s TV comedy *The Honeymooners*, the one where Mr. Manicotti dances the mambo. Waiting in his dressing room for a show to begin, Muddy would hear Rod Stewart's song coming over the house public address system. As if on cue, he'd get up out of his chair, swing his hips around and break into his little dance while singing, "Do you want my body," etc. Then he would just stand there and laugh and everybody would crack up along with him. I found it interesting that this legendary figure who rarely made comments about any songs on the radio was so irked by this one. He just couldn't believe that something like that could be a big hit.

Jump ahead to summer '79 and the three weeks we spent doing festivals in Europe. En route to our next show in France, Muddy and I were sitting in coach waiting for the plane to take off—Muddy on the aisle, his preferred seat, and me by the window. As we're waiting for boarding to be complete, this guy comes down the aisle, stops in front of us, and says: "Excuse me, I can't believe this." Mystery Man asks if he can have a few words with me. He looked nonthreatening, so I said okay. Muddy, ever the skeptic, wants to know what this is all about.

The guy looked at Muddy and said, "I know who you are, you're Muddy Waters." He then told us that he was with Jeff Beck—his road manager, or something like that. They're sitting up in first class and spotted us as we boarded the plane. He wanted to know if he could bring Beck back to meet the blues legend in coach. Muddy looked at me for some guidance on this one. I told him that Jeff Beck was a great guitar player, one of the best. Muddy consented. The go-between could bring him back, if he wanted to.

As the guy headed off to retrieve Beck, Muddy asked for more info on this guitar player who wanted to meet him, and I didn't have much time to bring Muddy up to speed. My knowledge of Jeff Beck was pretty much limited to the Yardbirds and the Jeff Beck Group of the 1960s. He's British, I told Muddy. One of the best, as good as Johnny Winter, as good as Clapton. I had to hope that would be enough info for purposes of a quick hello. Beck and his road manager were almost upon us. But no, Muddy wanted more. The only added detail that came to my mind was that Rod Stewart had been part of the Jeff Beck Group of the late sixties. I asked Muddy if he remembered the song "Da Ya Want My Body?"

He knew I was referring to Stewart's megahit "Da Ya Think I'm Sexy?" He kind of chuckled at that and said, "Oh, yeah." I tried to explain that the guitar player he was about to meet had played in a band with Stewart in the sixties. I knew Muddy had to process this information in record time, and I could only hope it would come out okay. The road manager came back with Beck and, needless to say, I was thrilled to meet him. Muddy reached out to shake Beck's hand and started off by complimenting him about being a great guitar player. So far so good. I was hoping that would end the encounter, but unfortunately Muddy plowed forward and my gut tightened. He mentioned knowing the chart-topper Beck made with his buddy, Rod Stewart. "You know the one! 'Do You Want My Body?'" Muddy wrapped it up with "nice to meet you."

I looked at a bewildered Jeff Beck and tried to imagine what the hell was going through his mind just then. Here this giant of British rock had come back to pay his respects to another music legend, and Muddy comes out with some off-the-wall reference to the song Muddy mockingly called "Do You Want My Body?"

I never bumped into Beck again, so I'll never know how he felt about that encounter. I hope he wasn't too offended. Muddy certainly meant no offense.

Although he could be awkward with the young stars playing in pop genres that bored him, and cantankerous even with musicians of his own kind, Muddy had a remarkably wide range of acquaintance among his musical peers, as I was already learning.

Chapter 15

BIG PICKS

Sometimes, Muddy would ask me to pick things up for him at a music store. Usually strings, thumb picks, finger picks. He used both types of picks. He liked National brand picks, the white ones, large size.

Muddy would say, "I got big fingers, so get me the large ones." When I came back with them, I would get him to try them on, to make sure they fit. They never did, according to Muddy, but he knew how to deal with that. He'd put them in a pot of boiling water until they got soft, then bend them onto his fingers.

Really? I had never heard of anyone doing that. I used a thumb pick on my guitar, but I would try picks on in music stores until I found one that fit me.

I was at Muddy's house one time and I saw him do it. Muddy was cooking, so we were in the kitchen. And, sure enough, he had a little pot of water boiling with a bunch of picks in it that I had bought him. I watched him fish out the picks. They were still mighty warm, but he put one on his forefinger and one on his thumb and started bending them. I guess he was on to something, because in all the shows I saw him do, never once did a pick come off his finger.

Chapter 16

BIG HEAD

Muddy often wore a hat in cold weather and so did I. One time I came back from a tour break wearing a new one I had picked up in New York. A "Big Apple cap." It was a pie-shaped hat, black. Muddy really dug it. He asked me where I got it and made it known that he would love to have one, too.

I told him I would look into it next time I was home. Make sure to get a large size, Muddy cautioned. He said he had a big head. I went home a few weeks later and ran over to the city, to the hat store on Eighth Avenue where I had gotten mine. Muddy had two different overcoats, one tweed and one camel hair, so I bought him a cap to match each, one tweed, one camel hair. Both extra big.

I mailed him the caps, and when they arrived he called to say thanks. To this day, I see pictures of Muddy wearing one of those caps, and I'm, like, yeah, I remember giving him that cap. It makes me feel good that he enjoyed them enough to actually wear them.

It was not the only thing of mine that Muddy seemed to covet, or pretended to. He really loved cars, Cadillacs above all. I picked up on that right away. One of his frequent observations when we were driving somewhere: "If you listen to the motor, it talks to you." He said that to me many times. If Muddy was flying into an airport in the northeast, I would sometimes pick him up in my car, a 1975 Buick Regal that I kept really clean. It had leather seats and the motor just purred. It was a really nice car.

The minute Muddy stepped into it, he had this routine. He would reach into his pocket and pull out a huge roll of cash. "How much you want for the car? I'll pay you right now." I'd tell him that I really

Muddy with "Big Apple cap." Photo by Brian O'Connor.
vHeritage Image Partnership Ltd./Alamy Stock Photo.

didn't want to sell the car. "It rides as good as a Cadillac," he'd tell me, and then ask again how much I wanted for it? "I really don't want to sell it." Elaborating on the fantasy, he'd say he wanted to drive the car back to Illinois and give it to his "Sunshine," meaning his wife, Marva. This became a funny routine—the wad of cash, the comments about how quiet the motor was—whenever I picked him up in the Buick. He really loved that car, but I never did sell it to him.

He had another little car thing going with John Lee Hooker. "John Lee Hooker got himself a Cadillac," he would say enviously. It was a lighthearted rivalry: which one of them had the better car? We were on a road trip, about a year into my time with Muddy, when he started talking about a car he had just bought, a yellow 1979 Lincoln Town Car.

When I finally got to see it, I had to agree it was beautiful, my idea of a very posh ride. Muddy called it "The Big Yellow Cat." The Cat had a leather interior with plush leather seats that felt like you were riding on a leather couch in your living room. It had a huge V8 motor that could either roar or purr, depending on how heavy your foot was. It had enough get-up to easily pass anything on the road, except a gas station.

Muddy was really proud of this car and would sometimes ask me to drive it. He noticed my habit of stepping on the gas when I rounded a curve. He would smile and say, "Oh, you give it a little gas when you go into the curve, I do the same thing." We agreed that when you could feel that curve, giving it a little gas would pull you through.

If Muddy and Pinetop were the antiques among us, their instruments also had some history. By the late seventies the vintage guitar market had started to boom. Old Fenders and Gibsons were getting hot. Everybody had an opinion about the different guitar models and brands, and prices were beginning to really skyrocket. Muddy had opinions, too. He would hear players talking about their instruments or me and Bob Margolin debating the fine points of various guitars. He'd chime in with this admonition: "And don't forget the amplifier because that's a big part of the sound too."

Muddy loved the Telecaster he bought new in 1958 ahead of his first trip to Europe. He nicknamed it "Hoss" and twenty years later it was as comfortable on him as a pair of old shoes. Muddy's amp— popular with a lot of guitar players—was a Fender Super Reverb. Before that he had used a 1950s Fender Bassman. (A Bassman was left behind in his house on Chicago's South Side when he moved to suburban Westmont.)

Willie Smith was living in the Chicago house when I first started working for Muddy. And Muddy's stepson Charles Williams (who wrote several songs Muddy recorded) was living in the basement.

Other alumni of the house included Otis Spann, Muddy's pianist from the 1950s until the late 1960s, and Paul Oscher, Muddy's harpist from 1967 into the early 1970s, the first white musician Muddy hired to be in his band. In previous years, the band rehearsed in the basement. Whenever I was at Willie's house, I'd go downstairs to visit Charles. Charles had traveled with the band in the past, helping Muddy and sometimes driving. I had gotten to know him even before I began working for Muddy. On my visits to the basement to say hi to Charles, I'd notice this raggedy old amp down there, Muddy's Fender Bassman. The tweed covering was long gone, replaced by some kind of reddish/orange contact paper. When I asked Muddy about it, he'd say, "Yeah, that's my amp that I used to use." Did he want me to fix it up for him? I'd have done it, but he never said yes. He didn't seem to care too much about it. I'd love to know what eventually happened to that amp—yet another thing that disappeared over the years. Someone told me later on that James Cotton (Muddy's harmonica player from the 1950s through the mid-1960s) had liked it. In fact, I think it's the one Cotton is using in the Muddy Waters video of his 1960 Newport performance. Also on that video: Pat Hare, the Memphis-based guitarist who recorded for Sun Records and was a sideman for Junior Parker, Howlin' Wolf, Bobby Bland, James Cotton, and others. Hare is playing the gold Les Paul that Muddy gave him.

At some point I came back from a road trip with Muddy with a new Les Paul of my own, a Les Paul Pro (Deluxe), black with cream colored P-90 pickups like the old Les Pauls, a really nice-looking guitar and quite heavy! Somebody mentioned it to Muddy, probably Bob Margolin or Fuzz Jones. I was settling into my hotel room when the phone rang. Muddy wanted to see the guitar and asked me to bring it to his room.

When I got there and opened the case, Muddy picked up the guitar, sat down and studied it. Not knowing where this was going or what he thought of my new axe, I was relieved to hear him say it was a beautiful guitar. He had had one in the fifties when they first came out, he told me. His was gold, but he agreed that they looked pretty in black. He asked me what I paid, and I told him: four hundred and change. About the same price he had paid for his, Muddy said, which kind of surprised me given how long ago that had been. Muddy started playing it, demonstrating how he used to "flip the switch— like this—and mess with the knobs down there" to get the beautiful tone he wanted. Muddy told me that after a while he had given his to Pat Hare, the guitarist and studio sideman whose love for power chords and distortion paved the way for both rockabilly and heavy metal. Pat was playing in Muddy's band in the early 1960s when he was sentenced to life behind bars for murdering his girlfriend and shooting the cop who came to investigate. An unrelated crime was almost as serious: Pat, while still a free man, had somehow broken the neck on the Les Paul that Muddy gave him. Twenty years later, I could see that Muddy was still pissed off about it. It would not be the last time the topic came up.

In June 1979, Muddy was opening for Eric Clapton at the Civic Center Arena in St. Paul, Minnesota, when Pat Hare was brought to the gig by a corrections officer. In the slammer, Hare had continued his musical career by starting a prison band called Sounds Incarcerated. Now in the terminal stages of lung cancer, he was permitted to sit down for a visit with Muddy ahead of the show. Right away they got back into it about the Les Paul. Muddy was still pissed off: "I gave you my Les Paul and you broke the neck on it." They went back and forth for a while, then settled down. I told Pat how much I liked his playing, and he seemed to appreciate that. I sat with him and the prison guard through Muddy's show. The best part was when Muddy called Pat to the stage to play "Got My Mojo Working."

Pat died a little over a year later, on September 26, 1980.

Muddy's tendency to hold a grudge for decades wasn't limited to Pat Hare. Another veteran of Muddy's band in the fifties was "Big Walter" Horton, the harmonica player. One night my friend Joe Berson brought Walter to one of Muddy's gigs just outside Chicago (Harry Hopes in Cary, Illinois).

Big Walter was still a regular on the scene in Chicago at that time and he had a lot of fans. Typically, he would walk into a venue, march up onto the bandstand, grab the mike, whip out his harp, and just start wailing. Didn't matter whose set it was. The crowd would recognize Horton and go crazy. Big Walter barging in like that wasn't to everybody's taste, but Joe had learned a lot from him about playing harmonica and seemed to feel loyal to him.

We were sitting in the dressing room with Muddy when, out of the blue, Walter offered to rejoin the band. "I just want you to know if you ever need me, just call me." Muddy reminded Walter that the last time he was supposed to come to a gig he didn't show up. As they went back and forth arguing a little more, I realized they were talking about some gig that happened in the 1950s, a quarter century ago, when Big Walter was in Muddy's band!

Now it's 1979, and Walter has a different take on why he didn't show up for the long-ago gig. "You fired me," he tells Muddy. Muddy fires back: "I didn't fire you, you just didn't show up. I had to get somebody else." I'm sitting there thinking, wow! How many years have gone by and they're still arguing about a club date in 1953, or whenever it was? Finally Walter laid the issue to rest by telling Muddy he was sorry and repeating that if he ever needed him to just let him know.

This business of quitting the band vs. getting fired would crop up again at a sad moment in the near future.

At Muddy's gigs, Walter wouldn't just walk up onto the stage and start playing, his usual routine. He would stand in front of Muddy, arms extended, and beseech him: "Let me play." Walter was really tall and often wore a long overcoat, making for a dramatic presence. It was a bizarre scene, and I'm sure Muddy's current harp player, Jerry Portnoy, did not appreciate it. But out of respect for Horton, he would graciously hand over the microphone and an old-timer would get to relive his glory days with a man he had crossed decades earlier.

Chapter 17

DUANE'S LES PAUL

You didn't have to break the neck of a guitar for an instrument to gain
the power of legend. That magic held true for me as much as anyone.
One of the first trips I did with Muddy took us into the Deep South
and on to Florida. It was April 1978. I flew to Chicago and drove with
the band down to Georgia. On April 7 and 8 we played Atlanta's Great
Southeast Music Hall. The Nighthawks, a blues-rock band based in
Washington, DC, opened for Muddy that night and were booked to
stay with us for a few more stops as we continued on to Florida. Much
to my surprise, they had an unannounced special guest on their show,
Gregg Allman. Muddy was very admiring of Gregg's vocals. "Oh, I
love the way Gregg sings," Muddy said to me one time. "He sings just
like a boy, just like a boy child." Muddy was responding to the soul
in Gregg's singing. He really dug him.

At one point during the Atlanta gig, Muddy called Gregg up on
stage to join us on the organ, which was right next to where I was
standing. Muddy kicked off a number and all of a sudden I saw Gregg
look up at me with a question mark in his eyes. He had hair all down
in front of his face and he kind of looked up from behind his hair and
said to me, "Hey, man, what key are we in?" I told him we were playing
in G. "Okay, thanks," he said. When the set was over, I was walking
down the hallway to Muddy's dressing room when a door opened
and the Allman Brothers' road manager, Twiggs Lyndon, stuck his
head out of Gregg's dressing room. There were a lot of stories about
Twiggs. I didn't know if they were true or not, but he was someone
that I figured I should stay away from.

"Hey, come here," Twiggs said. "I want to show you something." I figured it had to be drugs. "That's all right," I said. "There's some things I gotta do." But he insisted: "No, come in here. I want to show you something." So in I went, not knowing quite what to expect. Twiggs pointed to a guitar case on the floor. "Open that thing up. I want you to see something."

I was kind of thinking it might be something I really didn't want to see, but Twiggs was not to be denied. To my surprise, there was an old Sunburst Les Paul in there, a beauty. "Go ahead, pick it up, play it," Twiggs said. So I picked up the guitar and as I was putting it on my lap and getting ready to play a few chords, I see a name on the back of the guitar: "Duane," the Allman brother who had died in a motorcycle crash a few years earlier. It wasn't just written on it, it was spelled out in frets that had been hammered or glued in place. A bolt of lightning went off in my head. "I can't, I can't play this," I said. I handed the guitar back to Twiggs. "I saw Duane play this guitar. You gotta take it back, I can't play his guitar."

Twiggs said to me, "He'd want you to. It's okay, he'd want you to play it, why don't you take it up on the next set and play it with Muddy." I told him, thanks for the offer, but nah, the vibe is too strong coming from this guitar and I couldn't do it. Twiggs put the Les Paul back in the case, and that was that. Then in came Gregg. This must have been one of Gregg's kind of out-of-it periods. He sat down next to me on the dressing-room couch and at first I couldn't think what to say to him. Finally, I broke the silence with small talk: "I saw you play at the Fillmore East when you made that live Allman Brothers record. I was at that show and I'll never forget it."

He kind of pushed the hair out of his face, looked over at me, and says: "You were at that show?" And I said, "Yeah, I was there, it was the Allman Brothers, Johnny Winter, and Elvin Bishop." Gregg's face lit up. "Wow, you know, that was like my favorite show. That's when we used to play for like four hours." And I said, "Well, I think you played for two that night because there were other acts on the show. But it was a really great night and I'll never forget it."

Gregg kept saying to me, "Wow, you were at that show?" I told him I still had the program and the ticket stub. "Wow," he said again. Then he sort of went back into a dreamlike state, but for the moment, he had been very clear, also kind and polite. He seemed genuinely happy that I had been at that show and could talk about it with him.

Over the years I've often thought about what it would have been like playing Duane Allman's Les Paul with Muddy Waters, but I'm still convinced I made the right decision. Some things are sacred.

Chapter 18

MUDDY'S PIPE

Muddy used to call his slide "the pipe." He would say to me, "When I lay that pipe on them it's all over." He didn't care how many people were doing whatever, playing whatever, he didn't care who opened the show for him or if he was the opener. He knew that, when he played his slide solo, it was all over. People would go crazy. It was a guaranteed crowd pleaser. And he was so right. People loved that slide.

Muddy's slide was not store-bought. It was made for him by his old friend Andrew "Bo" Bolton. Bo and Muddy grew up together in Mississippi. Bo drove for Muddy at one time, and he also lived with Muddy at his homes in Chicago and in Westmont. Bo took care of things at home while Muddy was on the road. Sometimes he would drive me back to my hotel in Chicago after I returned a vehicle at the end of a road trip. Truth be told, I was kind of leery of Bo. He was not someone that I ever wanted to piss off. He was very quick with a knife, something that I saw him demonstrate more than once. You might be sitting around chatting idly with the guys and something would provoke him to pull out the blade. "I'll cut you," he'd snarl. Most of the time I think he was just fooling around. It scared the hell out of me, but he and Muddy were best buddies.

As for the slide Bo made, I wonder whatever happened to it. The story Muddy told me was that Bo used to work in a steel mill, and he made the slide from a flat piece of stainless steel that he heated and rolled to the exact size of Muddy's pinky—just the tip, not the whole finger. Muddy's name was engraved on it. As far as I know there were at least two of those slides. Muddy gave one to Fuzz Jones. I saw Fuzz using it one night in the dressing room, before a show. He was amusing Muddy by doing an imitation of his famous slide solo. And I have to say, he did it really well. I have no idea what happened to that slide either.

At some point Muddy mentioned to me that the Smithsonian had asked if he'd be willing to donate his red Telecaster to the museum, in Washington, DC, when he retired. This was before there was a Rock and Roll Hall of Fame or a Delta Blues Museum. My reaction was, wow! Muddy was being recognized as a part of American history and culture.

He told me that since the guitar was "kind of torn up," he wanted me to have it retouched. I pushed back. Did he really think he should do that? "Yeah," he said, "I don't want some raggedy guitar put in a museum." I understood where he was coming from. Muddy was a proud man. He was always well dressed, drove a nice car and kept a beautiful home. But this was different, I argued. The nicks and bruises were part of the guitar's history—Muddy's history. He wanted me to find someone who could "touch it up and make it look good." I suggested that he might want to think about that. The museum would probably want the guitar "as is." All the years of wear and tear only made it more interesting as a cultural relic. Muddy agreed to give it some more thought. Eventually the Telecaster wound up not at the Smithsonian but in the Rock and Roll Hall of Fame—without any touch-up.

Some years later—Muddy died in '83—I was touring with his son, Big Bill Morganfield. We were in Cleveland with a day off, so we went to check out the guitar at the Rock and Roll Hall of Fame. Bill introduced himself at the front door of the complex and they let us in—then explained somewhat sheepishly that Muddy's display had been taken down. There were plans to move it to the Buddy Holly Center, in Lubbock, Texas. Fortunately, the guitar and other items from the display were still in Cleveland, locked in a storage room. The gentleman we were dealing with was kind enough to give us a look. To my surprise, I actually got to hold Muddy's guitar. I never thought that would happen again! And the memories poured back into my head. As I inspected it, I explained to our guide what I knew about the guitar.

I immediately noticed that the bridge plate and saddles had been changed, replaced by a six-saddle gold or brass plated unit, and an extra string tree had been added. During my time with Muddy, the only change that happened—other than changing the strings every second night—was a fret job that I arranged through my childhood friend Jimmy Vivino. (Jimmy later became the bandleader for the Conan O'Brien TV show.) The work would be done by Tom (T. W.) Doyle, Les Paul's guitar tech. Muddy liked the idea: "If he's good enough for Les Paul he's good enough for me." The capo was replaced with a new one around the same time as the fret job, again at Muddy's request. (He gave me his old capo, and I still have it.) The guitar strap visible in photographs from 1979 on is one that I gave to Muddy, a black Martin Guitar strap embossed with an M. He loved that detail. Also missing: a flight case for the guitar that I bought for Muddy as a birthday present. I painted his initials (MW) on it in gold. It was made by a company called SMF Cases that Muddy referred to as "Some Mother Fucker."

After leaving the Hall of Fame storage locker, I tried to find out who made the changes to Muddy's guitar, and where the missing parts might be. No luck. The last photo I saw of the guitar was from 2017 and it appeared that the original parts were back in place, though I suppose they could have been reproductions. I was never able to find out who did the restoration, but I'm glad they did it.

Chapter 19

A TOAST TO ALL THAT

It wasn't all diner eggs and Pancake Houses. Muddy definitely knew how to throw a bash. On his birthday, April 4, 1979—either his sixty-fourth or sixty-sixth—we were in Missouri, staying at the Rodeway Inn in Springfield. (Muddy always referred to Rodeways as "Roachway Inns.") The hotel marquee was emblazoned with the words, "Happy Birthday, Muddy Waters." Muddy's wife, family, and some friends came down from Chicago for the party in a banquet hall Muddy had reserved. There were tables set up for the guests, and in each corner of the room were sixty-four-gallon trash cans filled with ice and champagne. Three of them were stocked with Piper-Heidsieck. The barrel closest to Muddy's table was filled with bottles of Dom Perignon.

The champagne was chilling, the steaks were cooking, and Muddy was clearly enjoying himself. He watched in some astonishment as Jerry Portnoy, the band's most ravenous carnivore, inhaled his first steak. Jerry must have muttered something about wanting another, to which Muddy graciously replied: "If you can eat it, go ahead on." Whereupon Portnoy wolfed down a second steak. Then a third. At one point I went over to Muddy's table to wish him happy birthday. I raised my glass of champagne, which tasted pretty damn good, I must say. Muddy thanked me and then asked what I was drinking. I told him Piper-Heidsieck, the usual. But this was a special occasion. He told me to finish what was in my glass, then reached for his nearby bottle of Dom Perignon. "Let's drink some of the good shit," he said, refilling my glass and clicking his against it. It was a birthday toast, but in my mind it was a salute to this whole era in my life and the privilege of working with Muddy Waters. "Good shit," indeed!

Chapter 20

LITTLE MAN, HUGE VOICE

One time while on a break in our touring schedule, I went back east for a family visit. While there I called Muddy, just to check in with him and see how he was doing. He told me he was okay and asked what I was up to. I told him I was going to go see James Brown that night. I wasn't sure how Muddy would react to that. Muddy had the utmost respect for the top blues and jazz artists we encountered at festivals and on the road, but James Brown—singer, dancer, musician? The "Godfather of Soul" might be a bit much for a traditionalist. They were playing the Lone Star Café in downtown Manhattan. Muddy's reply surprised me. "James Brown, old soldier, you tell him I said hello." I went to the show, but didn't get to tell him that Muddy had sent his regards to the "old soldier." I took it as a sign of deep respect.

Muddy once told me a story about a show he was on with Percy Mayfield, the great singer/songwriter. Mayfield had written numbers made famous by Ray Charles and many others. I had heard Muddy say how much he liked the man's deep, soulful voice. And he liked his songs too. I was a big fan of Percy Mayfield but had never had a chance to see him in person, so I wanted to hear Muddy's story.

Backstage ahead of the show, Muddy put out the word that he would like to meet Mayfield. He was cooling his heels in the dressing room when someone knocked on the door. Muddy: "Who is it?" A very deep voice on the other side: "It's Percy Mayfield." Muddy opens the door, sees this slender guy standing out there, and says, "Well, where'd he go?" He glances up and down the hallway looking for the hulking man he figured you'd have to be to have a voice as deep as Mayfield's. The man at the door set him straight: "I'm Percy Mayfield."

They chatted amiably for a while. A few years later I found myself on a show with Mayfield. And as I looked forward to hearing that resonant voice, I recalled Muddy's story. The minute this lean fellow took the stage I understood why Muddy had been so surprised when he met Percy Mayfield. And then he opened up and started singing, and, oh, that voice!

In July 1979, I was in France with Muddy for La Grande Parade du Jazz, now known as the Nice Jazz Festival, a great mix of blues and jazz acts. During daytime hours, Muddy would pretty much stay in his hotel room and I'd venture out to hear the sounds. When I saw that Lionel Hampton was playing the festival with an all-star band, I decided to check him out. I also wanted to see band member Arnett Cobb, the legendary tenor sax player from Texas, last encountered when he sat beside me on the flight to Europe and helped himself (and me) to splits of gin from the flight attendant's cart. After the show—a class act, in my view—I told Muddy about seeing Hampton. I was uncertain how he would respond. Muddy played a very different kind of music, but he had a lot of friends among the top jazz masters. For example, Dizzy Gillespie would usually sit in if he and Muddy were playing the same festival.

I had to wonder if that same kind of friendship would extend to an urbane cat like Hampton, celebrated for his prowess with percussion and, above all, vibes. Turned out it did. When I mentioned seeing him, Muddy said, "Oh, Hamp, you tell Hamp that I said hello to him." The next day, I'm strolling around the festival and who should I run into but Lionel Hampton. I told him I worked for Muddy Waters and that Muddy said to say hello. Hampton's eyes just kind of lit up and he broke into a big smile. "Muddy Waters! Well you tell him that Hamp says hello, too." It was mutual respect. A lot of jazz guys didn't really have that much interest in the blues, either the Delta variety or the electrified Chicago sound. But they all respected Muddy.

If I were trying to make a complete list of the musicians Muddy held in high esteem, I'd have to include John Hammond Jr. Muddy respected him as a guitar player and a man, and John had the deepest respect for the older bluesmen.

It was on Hammond's recommendation that Muddy contacted the Rosebud Agency in San Francisco. We were doing a festival with John when I heard Muddy talking to him in the dressing room and venting frustration with his then current agency. At the time Muddy was having a lot of problems with booking agencies; I'm sure he did throughout his career. In the few years I was with Muddy he went through two different ones (Paragon Agency, out of Macon, Georgia, and New York City–based F.B.I., Frontier Booking International) before signing with Rosebud. Hammond gave Muddy the name of Mike Kappus at Rosebud, saying he had had a very positive experience with him. Muddy had his manager, Scott Cameron, get in touch with Rosebud and soon Muddy was a client. Things got much better once Rosebud took over the bookings. I know Muddy was relieved to have an agency that he could finally trust.

Willie Dixon and John Lee Hooker also found their way to Rosebud, making it the premier agency for blues legends. John Hammond Jr. deserves credit for being the catalyst who helped these great artists get better bookings.

Chapter 21

REHASHING AN OLD LYRIC

Muddy wasn't writing much music during the years when I was around. But sometimes I could get him going about the era when he did a lot of it. One time he told me a story about his 1951 recording "She Moves Me" (Chess 1490).

He had been in a barbershop getting his hair done, Muddy told me, when the barber spotted a woman walking by and just went crazy. He kept looking at her and saying, "She moves me, she moves me!" Muddy built the song around that.

When I asked him how come he wasn't writing anymore, his answer was interesting. Writing songs is a young person's game, he said. When you get older your mind changes. And you don't have that spark in there for writing songs like you did when you were young. The ideas stop coming to you, and you start to be concerned about other things in your life.

Being still young myself, a guy in his twenties, I couldn't relate to that. When I first started with Muddy he was sixty-two years old, I was twenty-two. Now that I'm in my sixties, with my own life experiences, Muddy's story makes sense to me.

I knew about some of the "other things" that had crowded songwriting out of Muddy's life. Music is a tough business, and Muddy wasn't always happy with the wheeling and dealing. There was constant pressure to keep the band working, because all the guys had families. Not to mention Muddy's need to take care of his own family.

And then there were health issues that had started to crop up, heart disease among them. They also weighed on his mind. He kept most of it private, but once in a while he would mention his blood pressure and that he couldn't drink because the doctor had put him on some medication. That said, he would pull a bag of weed out of his pocket and ask me to roll it up for him. Muddy loved his reefer.

If Muddy had pretty much completed his songbook by the time I knew him, that's not to say he didn't adapt it to the needs of a widening audience.

Before the tour with Clapton, Muddy had been working on the song "Champagne & Reefer," which was included on an album he did for Blue Sky Records called *King Bee*, his last recording. He played around with the words for a while. Sometimes when I met him coming off of a plane, the first words out of his mouth would be: "Hey, write this down." And I'd whip out a pencil and the little notepad I carried with me. It was interesting to watch him put a song together. I remember questioning him about the line where he says "I'm gonna get high just as sure as my name." Muddy told me "sure as my name" was a strong way of saying "without a doubt." He tweaked the lyrics again and again, sometimes flipping a couple of verses, until he got the song just the way it had to be to become a crowd pleaser.

I know a lot of people thought "Champagne & Reefer" was a sellout kind of song, but it was something he actually put a lot of thought into and, hey, this was the seventies. There was a lot of weed around, and Muddy did like his champagne. "Champagne & Reefer" became a regular part of Muddy's shows. "Bring me champagne when I'm thirsty, bring me a reefer when I want to get high," the lyrics went, and the response would be instant. People would cheer, and sometimes throw joints at the stage.

But not in Europe. On the Clapton tour in late 1978, the song drew no response at all. Muddy was mystified. One night, as I was sitting there watching the show from the side of the stage, it dawned on me what might be going wrong. In Europe they smoked hashish, not "reefer"! I asked Muddy if he would be willing to swap the word "hash" for the word "reefer." Muddy looked at me kind of funny: "Hash?" That's what they smoke over here, I told him. They roll it up with tobacco. Muddy said what the hell, he'd rework the lyric and give it a try.

So for the next show, when Muddy got to the tweaked line—"Bring me some HASH when I want to get high"—he hammered the word "hash." Sure enough, people started clapping and cheering. These shows were mostly in big arenas in front of thousands of people, so the crowd's approval quickly swelled to a roar. Muddy tried it for a few nights and got the same response. He thanked me for my suggestion and stayed with the revamped lyric for the rest of the tour, happy that the song was getting over again.

Another song that kind of bombed in Europe was the one called "Howlin' Wolf." The words go "I'm a howlin' wolf, I'm howlin' all around your door." By contrast, I noticed that another of Muddy's songs, "They Call Me Muddy Waters," drew a roar of approval the minute Muddy sang his own name.

Some of the guys in the band picked up on this, just as I had. I took it upon myself to suggest that maybe he should drop "Howlin' Wolf" and substitute "They Call Me Muddy Waters," which is what he did for the rest of the tour.

The point being that, stubborn as Muddy could be, if he heard something that made sense to him (a song suggestion occasionally from someone in the band or even from me) he sometimes would listen to us and try it out. I was honored that he allowed me to give him an opinion, but, as always, you had to present your thoughts tactfully. I would dare to suggest that in the hurly-burly of performing live, he might not be picking up on how the crowd was reacting. He would usually be comfortable with that approach. He was definitely more interested in crowd response than in hearing my views on the quality of this lyric versus that one.

Chapter 22

A FACE IN THE WINDOW

Muddy was sternly against any sort of hard drugs, any kind of powder. Cocaine? He was totally against it, and there was a lot of it around in the seventies. Sometimes as he came offstage on his way to the dressing room someone would slip something into his pocket, a little vial with powder in it, perhaps. He would immediately pull it out and look at me: "What the hell is this?" Back then, plenty of people would have been happy to partake. Muddy would get rid of it immediately. He didn't want anything to do with it. Weed? That was different—no big deal. He smoked it from time to time—usually if he was on some medication and couldn't drink—and probably had been doing so since the fifties. He thought it was really stupid that it was illegal, given the other things out there that were far more dangerous.

Occasionally he would call me to his room to roll some joints for him. It cracked me up the way he handled a joint. He would never smoke it down too far because he worried about burning his fingers. Muddy would light up a joint, smoke it about halfway down, pass it off to somebody else, and light up another. Once he achieved his desired buzz, he was done. There would be no liquor for him that night. He'd drink a glass of water instead.

Pot didn't seem to bring out the devil in Muddy the way the Hennessy had. He didn't zap bad vibes at some member of the band who had irked him that evening, the way he did after topping off champagne with a nip of brandy. Sometimes he'd be feeling pretty good from the smoke before a show and go out on the stage holding a glass of water in his hand. He had the water in case his mouth was too dry to sing. Sometimes when he came off the stage, he'd say to me that he was so high when he got out there that he had to feel his way around to find his stool. Muddy had taken to sitting down while he played ever since his traffic accident in the late sixties. I only saw him stand for a show once, in Pendleton, Oregon, in May 1978. It was an outdoor show at the Round-Up Grounds. Muddy was opening for Elvin Bishop, the guitar player—an alumnus of the Paul Butterfield Blues Band—whose own group was riding high following their hit two years earlier, "Fooled Around and Fell in Love." It was so cold that Muddy kept his overcoat on while playing the entire forty-five-minute set.

Not that weed was totally problem-free. Once in a while when I picked Muddy up at the airport, he'd tell me that his doctor had put him on some new medicine and he couldn't drink anything. On more than one occasion this news was followed by him reaching into his jacket pocket and pulling out a bag of weed. "When we get to the hotel you gotta roll this up for me," he'd say. Back then there wasn't the level of security that there is today, but I would panic seeing him pull a bag out in the middle of an airport terminal. I'd tell him to put it away. What are you doing?! Muddy would wander right through the airport with a bag in his pocket. Nobody bothered him.

For one of Muddy's "can't drink tonight" nights, we were at the State Theater in Newark, Delaware (August 17, 1979). He was enjoying a joint in the dressing room, a floor above the stage, while the band warmed up the crowd. After a few minutes I noticed Muddy's eyes fixed on the window. It was dark outside so we hadn't realized there was a fire escape landing just beyond it. "Somebody's out there," Muddy insisted. I thought it was probably the pot putting him a little on edge, but I figured I'd better check it out. I went over to the window and looked into the darkness but couldn't see anything. "I'm telling you somebody's out there," Muddy said again. I looked again, saw nothing. I took a seat beside Muddy and was trying to calm him when the window started opening. Sure enough, there was somebody on the fire escape. The window opened the rest of the way and this unknown dude said, "Hello," and walked through the dressing room and off to parts unknown.

Muddy said to me: "I told you somebody was out there." And after that, anytime Muddy told me he saw something—whether buzzed on weed or otherwise—I never doubted him.

Chapter 23

THE ROLLS-ROYCE OF INTERVIEWS

I sat in on a lot of Muddy's interviews. If one was scheduled, I would get word from Cameron's office or from Scott himself to handle the get-together. By the time I was working with him, Muddy had been doing interviews for over thirty years and was a bit tired of being asked the same questions for the umpteenth time. He basically looked to do as little as possible during an interview—maybe five minutes, or something like that.

Occasionally Cameron's management team would agree to something longer, but would caution the interviewer that Muddy usually wasn't good for more than a quickie. One of the questions he would be asked too often: Now that he was comfortable in his life could he still really sing the blues? Muddy wasn't struggling any longer; he wasn't wealthy but he was comfortable for sure. He had a ready answer: "Can I still sing the blues? Sure, I got a long memory."

Muddy had worked out a way to signal to me that five minutes was up and it was time to wind things down. He'd pull on his earlobe. I'd start watching for the signal around the five-minute mark. There were those rare occasions when Muddy got comfortable with an interviewer and would take questions for ten minutes, fifteen minutes. But most times, I'd see him start yanking on that earlobe, and I knew it was time to get the interviewer out of his face. Fast!

The Clapton tour got us to London for several dates over about ten days. At one point the BBC contacted me about having Muddy do an interview for BBC Radio 1. Muddy agreed to it and we were told they'd send a car to pick us up. On the appointed day, I met Muddy in the hotel lobby. We had been sitting there for quite a while when Muddy said, "You better go check and see if there's a car out there."

So, I looked outside. Remember, Muddy was super conscious about being on time. We were definitely on time, but where the hell was the BBC car? I noticed a Rolls-Royce parked in front of the hotel. That was the only car out there.

So, we sat in the lobby and continued to wait. Every few minutes, Muddy would say to me, "You better go see if that car has come yet." I would step out of the hotel and take another look. And there would still be just one car, the Rolls-Royce. "You think they'd send a Rolls for us, Mud?" I was joking. Muddy looked at me like I was either stoned or stupid. "A Rolls-Royce? Ain't no way in hell they'd send a Rolls-Royce for us. You better call that radio station and see where their car is."

So, I said to Muddy, "Just for kicks I'm going to go out and see if there's a driver in that car. I'm going to go out and tap on the window, and find out what the deal is with that car." So Muddy said, "You're wasting your time, they ain't going to send no Rolls-Royce for us."

I made my way outside. It's early December and it's cold. I tapped on the window of the Rolls-Royce, the window rolled down and I asked the driver, "Are you waiting here to pick someone up?" And he replied, "Yeah, I'm waiting here to pick up Muddy Waters." This was going to make Muddy's day—mine, too. "I'll go get him right now," I told the driver.

I found Muddy back in the hotel lobby. "Hey, Muddy, guess what?" I said. "That Rolls-Royce is for you." He looked at me in disbelief. "What! They sent the Rolls-Royce for me?" I said, "Yeah, we better go, we're late." So off we went, in a Rolls. Muddy loved cars, and as we sat in the lap of luxury, this really plush back seat, I could see he was one happy bluesman. He kept admiring the fine wood and leather interior. "Oh, man, this a beautiful car." He said he dreamed of owning one.

Rolls-Royce or no Rolls-Royce, as we sat in the BBC studio waiting for the interview to begin, I had every expectation that five minutes in, Muddy would start pulling on his earlobe. Or I'd pull on mine, which was how I signaled that an interview was going nowhere and it was time to leave. This interview defied my expectations.

All of a sudden, the interviewer (who I believe was the late John Peel) started playing Muddy's old 78s and asking him really great questions about different songs. I looked at Muddy after several minutes went by and started pulling on my earlobe a little bit. Muddy shook his head, no.

He was enjoying himself. More songs were played, the conversation continued. After fifteen minutes or so, there was a break. I turned to Muddy: "Do you want me to get you out of here?" "No," he said, "This is a good interview, this guy is asking me some good questions."

The whole interview probably took thirty or forty minutes, the longest I ever saw Muddy do. And when it was over, we got back into the Rolls like it was ours and headed back to the hotel.

Chapter 24

ANOTHER STONE ROLLS BY

Playing road manager had its ups and downs, but the worst of it was a small price to pay for a young white guy thrilled by those moments when I got to join a living legend named Muddy Waters on stage. There were other creative opportunities that came with my job and some of them could be almost as satisfying. We were about two weeks into the Clapton tour when we arrived in Glasgow, Scotland, on November 24, 1978. That's when I noticed Ian Stewart, the Rolling Stones' piano player, roaming around backstage at the Apollo Theatre. He was there to see Eric and Muddy. We chatted a bit in the dressing room before the show. He seemed friendly, a no-nonsense kind of guy.

One of the advantages of being road manager was that I always had access to Muddy. I would mention artists who were in the house. Some he might have known or heard of, others maybe not. Some would ask to sit in, some just wanted to say hello. As pianists go, Ian Stewart was someone special. I had seen him several times with the Stones and thought he would mesh beautifully with Muddy's band. And so I began lobbying. I knew Pinetop Perkins would be okay with it because it was rare that someone asked to sit in on piano. It was usually harmonica players asking to sit in. Now it was time to ask Ian, which I did the next time we got to chatting backstage. He didn't hesitate for a split second. He said he'd love to do it. I excused myself and ducked into the dressing room to tell Muddy that the Rolling Stones' piano player was in the house and would like to sit in if possible.

Muddy said yes. Then he asked me Ian's name and repeated it a couple of times to make sure he had it right. I made my way back to

Ian to let him know that Muddy was on board and would call him up on stage at some point in the set. Which he did, except that in typical Muddy fashion, instead of calling Ian by name, he ordered "the Rolling Stones piano player to come on up here!"

Ian took the stage and played dazzlingly, as usual. Coming off the stage, he thanked me for making it happen and I thanked him for doing it.

Once in a while it was nice to be in a position where I could kind of instigate something like that—something that was good for everyone involved, something everyone could enjoy. Me, too!

Chapter 25

WHY STOP NOW?

Toward the end of the tour, I learned from Clapton's manager that they had an American tour coming up the following spring, a pretty long one, maybe eight or nine weeks.

Muddy and all the band had really enjoyed opening for Clapton. It was just great to be part of a sold-out tour through Europe and Britain. The one downside was the chilly bus, but at least on a bus we could get up and move—a far cry from the cramped Suburbans we had in the states. Plus, we didn't have to drive! Muddy appreciated how Clapton's huge audiences were helping him career-wise. He enjoyed Eric's company and the band loved being an opening act, a forty-five-minute set that was over by 9:00 each night.

When I mentioned Clapton's upcoming American tour, Muddy was hot to be part of it. I suggested that he talk to Eric directly and let him know. Muddy thought that was a good idea but wondered how he'd be received.

I said I was confident that if Eric heard the request coming from him, it would be hard for him to say no. Okay, Muddy said, but when should he pop the question? I asked Muddy for time to think about it.

Jerry Portnoy and I had roomed together for the entire five weeks we were in Europe, and he was very helpful to me in strategizing ways to make the US tour happen. I was also very fortunate to have a representative from CBS on hand in London. Barry Humphries represented Blue Sky Records in the UK and would call me regularly to ask if there was anything he and CBS (Blue Sky's distributor in the UK) could do for Muddy. I would thank him and promise to let him know if anything came up. Now it occurred to me that maybe we needed to create a setting for Muddy to be with Eric, where everyone would be in a great mood—a party!

Muddy was really good at throwing parties, as I knew from having been at more than a few of them, including his birthday and that backstage party with the Rolling Stones. He got relaxed and talkative at these events, making the prospect of a party with Clapton far superior to just walking up to him and asking if he could be on the next tour. It dawned on me that maybe this could be something a little more formal, not just a backstage gathering. How about a dinner party for Eric and his manager and crew? I mentioned the calls I'd been getting from Humphries and said I bet CBS could make it happen. Muddy was all in.

So that's how it came down. I called Barry and told him Muddy wanted to have a dinner party in appreciation of Eric and his manager for putting him on the tour. And it would be a way to thank the crew for all they did for us. The CBS rep thought it was a great idea and asked me to come up with the number of guests who would be attending. At first it looked like about thirty people. I had to add a few more, and CBS wanted some of their people there, too. All told we got the guest list above forty.

Humphries put together a really impressive party in a wonderful London restaurant that they rented out for the evening. The CBS people took care of all the details, the menu, the champagne for Muddy, all I had to do was figure out the seating for the main table, a table for ten.

I wanted to make sure that Muddy and Eric were next to each other. And that Eric's manager, Roger Forrester, was right there with them. Muddy had some thoughts of his own. He wanted me to be directly across the table from him, and when I felt the vibes were right, he wanted me to pull on my earlobe. That meant it was time for Muddy to tell Eric and Roger that he wanted to be on their US tour. Next to Eric I put Pattie Boyd, the former Mrs. George Harrison, who would soon marry Clapton. Forrester and his wife were on Muddy's other side. The other four seats were CBS people.

Pattie was, of course, a legendary beauty, a fascinating and, for me, somewhat intimidating presence. She had been around during the tour, polite but very quiet. She would say hello and that was about it. She seemed to be in her own world, a mystery. But now here I was sitting across from her, trying to think of what to say while simultaneously monitoring Muddy and Eric to see when to pull my earlobe and cue Muddy to pop the question.

The party was wonderful and Muddy was clearly enjoying himself. He would glance over at me every so often to see if now was the time. But since things were just getting under way, I wanted to wait until I saw that Muddy, Eric, and Roger had tuned out the rest of us and were deep in conversation. Several times I looked at Muddy and shook my head. No, it wasn't the right time yet.

Meanwhile, to my surprise, Pattie started talking to me. This came as a relief since I had been unsure what I should say to her or if she wanted to talk to me at all. She talked about the Maharishi and going to India in the sixties. It took me a minute to register that she was talking about the Beatles interlude with the Maharishi and that she had been there with them.

In this party kind of setting, a social gathering, she seemed to really come alive, telling me stories and messing with me a bit. At one point she held up her cigarette pack, Camels, and asked me a question that turned out to be more like a riddle. If you were in the desert with this camel and suddenly a storm blew in, where would you take shelter?

I'm sure I came up with some lame answer—I'd hide under the camel, or something like that. I don't remember what it was, but I remember she burst out laughing. "I would check into the hotel around the corner," she said, rotating the pack in her hand to reveal the building on the other side. She had a good laugh on me, but I didn't mind. Pattie was more than charming.

When it was time for dessert, they served up something called Christmas pudding, which I had never had before. It didn't look like any kind of pudding that I knew. Seeing that I was baffled by this confection, Pattie went into detail, explaining that the pudding was an old English tradition that was only made once a year, around

Christmas. She said it was a very elaborate thing to make because of all the ingredients needed, and a real treat to eat. To me it tasted like a warm, extra rich fruitcake with some brandy mixed in. And yes, it was mmm-mmm good.

Amid these pleasant distractions, I still had to stay focused on Muddy and spot the right moment for him to ask Eric and Roger about our joining the US tour. The moment came at the end of the dinner as Muddy, Eric. and Roger talked together. At that moment, I made eye contact with Muddy and gave him the high sign, a tug on my earlobe. Muddy nodded to me, turned to Eric, and told him he really wanted to be on his upcoming US tour. He then turned to Roger and said the same thing. Eric and Roger both seemed receptive to the idea and soon we had the official greenlight.

Muddy was really happy about the way that dinner turned out.

And needless to say, I was too. After all, we got the tour!

Chapter 26

NO OFFENSE, GEORGE

Eric liked to do the occasional show near where he lived and the last one on our tour with him was in Guildford, a large town in Surrey, southwest of central London. It was in a smallish venue called the Civic Hall on December 7. Footage from this show made it into the documentary *Eric Clapton's Rolling Hotel*. I played that night but it's not in the film. Instead they spliced in a clip from another show with me playing on "Got My Mojo Working."

I was sitting in the dressing room waiting to go on with Muddy when Eric walked in with George Harrison. Cool! This is going to be real interesting, I thought to myself: Muddy meets a Beatle. But I had to wonder if he would have any idea who this guy was.

Eric's introduction wasn't necessarily going to do the job: "Muddy, I'd like you to meet a friend of mine. This is George." Muddy sticks out his hand: "Well, hey man, nice to meet you." Muddy paused for a moment. He was looking at Harrison intently, and then the light-bulb went on—part way. "Hey, you one of the Beatles. You one of the Beatles, ain't you?" Harrison: "Well, I used to be." I will never forget Muddy's response: "You the piano player, right?"

I'm sure Muddy respected the colossal success the Beatles had enjoyed, but he had not closely followed their music. Harrison kind of chuckled: "I play guitar." Muddy had another question: "Where's the rest of your boys?" I tried not to start laughing. "I don't know," Harrison said, "I haven't seen them in ten years." Muddy processes that, and then says, "Well, don't you think it's about time you all got back together again?" It was an innocent question, but ignorant of the

102

Beatles' ruptures and schisms and repeated efforts to patch things up. With that, George and Eric chuckled and eased on out of the room. After the set was over, I went back to the dressing room to relax and who should walk back in but George Harrison. I'm just sitting there, winding down over a glass of spirits, when he comes over to me. I'm kind of flabbergasted. A Beatle has zeroed in on little ol' me. He leans over my chair and sticks out his hand, and says, "Hello, my name is George." Me: "I know who you are." Harrison: "You mind if I ask you a few questions?"

I'm thinking: Here's one for the boys back in Jersey. George Harrison wants to ask me a few questions. "Sure," I said, "you can ask me whatever." Here's what was on Harrison's mind: "Well, you know I play slide guitar, and I was watching Muddy play slide, and I was wondering how he gets that sound. I didn't see him plugged into any kind of effects box. It looks like he's plugged straight into the amp. So how does he get that sound?" I said to him, "Well, that's easy. I can answer that for you."

George looked at me like I was offering him a sip from the holy grail. I was going to reveal the secret of Muddy's tone. I wasn't trying to be a wise guy, I just wanted to give him an honest answer: "I can tell you how he gets that sound." I held up my left hand and said, "He uses this hand," then I held up on my right hand and said, "He uses this hand and he can get it on any guitar."

George kind of looked at me and made no comment. I went on: "It's his hands. His sound, it's his hands." George kept looking at me, looking like he was a little puzzled. It wasn't the answer he was expecting. So I told him a personal story: One time Muddy played my Fender Stratocaster and it sounded like he was playing his own guitar. He got his classic sound. Muddy played a Telecaster, but in his hands he made my Stratocaster sound the way he always sounds. I told Harrison I was so freaked out that I took my guitar, put it in the case and didn't touch it for six months. I guess George was satisfied with the answer because he thanked me.

We talked a little longer, mostly about guitar players. He told me I was a good young player and I let him know that, coming from him, it was a wonderful compliment. I told him I really admired all the Chet Atkins and Carl Perkins country stuff he played. At one point he asked me if I ever got tired of playing those same three chords, the ones that make the blues blue. Not meaning to sound like a wise guy, I said no, sometimes we only play two. With that he kind of looked at me and backed out of the room.

I must say he was very polite, probably the nicest rock star I ever talked to.

There you have it, George Harrison asking me how Muddy gets his tone. George Harrison always had great tone, but I always wished that there was another opportunity to talk with him and clarify one thing. I wasn't trying to be a wise guy. That was really the way Muddy got that sound, it was his hands.

Chapter 27

INCIDENTAL EXPENSES

At the end of the five-week tour with Clapton, I got a message at our hotel in London from Roger Forrester, Eric's manager. He wanted me to call his office at the Robert Stigwood Organisation. I did that and was instructed to show up in person. So, I took a cab to the address they gave me. I had no idea why I was being summoned to Roger's office. I hoped it didn't have to do with the US tour that he and Eric had just agreed to, but I couldn't think of anything else Roger would want to speak to me about. On arrival, I was brought into Roger's office and told to sit down. It's a good thing I was sitting down. I was not prepared for what I was about to hear. Roger started talking about expenses incurred by Muddy during the tour just completed. Expenses? What expenses? And he said: "Well, yeah, there's transportation, equipment rental . . ." I began to squirm as he went on itemizing the charges. He had a list of them and he wanted us to repay every pence, pound, franc, and deutschmark. I don't remember the exact number the expenses came to, but I freaked out. It was a substantial piece of change and I did not relish being the one who would have to deliver the bad news to Muddy.

I told Roger that I didn't understand why this was happening. He must have sensed that I was coming apart because he offered me a shot of brandy to settle my nerves. I downed the shot. Muddy was not going to be happy about this, I warned. Given how little we were making on the tour, Muddy certainly wasn't expecting to be hit up for a bunch of incidental expenses. I had always liked and respected Forrester, but on this occasion, he was unbending. He told me to deliver the message to Muddy and, with that, he showed me out. So there I was, saddled with the task of being the messenger bearing some really bad news. This wasn't going to be pretty. Muddy was going to be pissed, furious. Out on the street I hailed a taxi back to the hotel. There was no good way to present the bad news to Muddy, but it had to be done.

As soon as I got to the hotel, I called Muddy's room and told him we needed to talk. He knew I had gone to Roger's office for some kind of a meeting and feared, as I had, that they might have decided against bringing us on the US tour. "What's going on?" Muddy asked. Fortunately he was sitting down—but not for long. I told him about the list of expenses that Forrester wanted reimbursed. I mentioned the total—whatever it was. Muddy bolted up from his seat, and this I will never forget. He puts a hand over his heart and roars at me: "The man is a bullshitter from his heart! From his heart! You tell him to go fuck himself! I ain't payin' him a dime. Tell him to FUCK HIMSELF!"

I didn't tell Roger to go fuck himself and I didn't tell him he was a "bullshitter from his heart." But what I did tell him, when I got back to him, was that Muddy was very upset and was not going to pay. "He can't understand how these charges happened at all," I added. Muddy couldn't wrap his head around the fact that he was invited to join this tour with Eric and was happy and grateful for the opportunity, but there was no discussion in advance about charges he might be responsible for.

Maybe Blue Sky Records or CBS London wound up repaying Forrester for whatever those expenses were. Or maybe Eric found out and covered for us. That phone call was the last I ever heard about them. The matter got cleared up—or just dropped—and that was the end of that. But the incident left Muddy with a really bad taste in his mouth. He knew Roger was a figure far more powerful than his own manager, Scott Cameron, but he had lost respect for him and never trusted him again. The US tour went on as scheduled, and ended without a hitch, but even after that success, Muddy was reluctant to have further dealings with Roger.

After the last show on the overseas part of the Clapton tour, Eric decided to throw a party. Muddy and everyone in the band got on our bus and headed over to Eric's house, not far from where we had played. Upon arrival I noticed some mighty nice cars parked outside, very high end. Elton John was there but a little standoffish, as though he was still smarting from the door in his face when he tried to visit Muddy's dressing room in New York, and also from earlier that evening in Guildford as Muddy was exiting the stage and again failed to acknowledge the Rocket Man.

George Harrison was at the party, too, and once again Harrison and I fell to chatting. I asked him what he was up to and he told me about an album he was recording. In London? No, he was recording it at his house. I mentioned how nice it must be to have a studio in your house. Just then his gaze shifted across the room to where Eric was talking with Pattie, Harrison's ex-wife.

"Eric's my best friend," Harrison said. "I just love him." I remember thinking to myself that this was really kind of amazing. I'm standing here talking to George Harrison. Pattie and Eric are standing nearby. Pattie is George's ex-wife and his best friend's lover. It astonished me to hear Harrison say how much he loved them both. Pattie was this incredible woman who was a big part of their lives, past and present. She had inspired some of the best songs either of them had written and they were still friends. It kind of blew my mind.

There was a piano in Eric's party room and before too long Pinetop Perkins settled in and started serenading the ladies. I think it was the same room pictured on the US cover of the Blind Faith album, with Eric and his buddies standing around holding instruments. Muddy was having a great time, and was impressed by Eric's digs, a substantial house in a wealthy area outside London. Muddy lived about the same distance from another world-class city, Chicago, but in a much more modest house. As Muddy and I chatted, I mentioned the vast size of Eric's house and was surprised by his response. Yes, the place was grand and beautiful, Muddy agreed, but he added that he wouldn't want it. I had to know why. It was too big, Muddy said, he would never know who was home. Muddy preferred his own place, with his seat by the kitchen window and its view of the front door and anyone who came in or went out.

As the party wound down, we said our goodbyes and headed over to our bus for the ride back to London. As usual, I had a hard time getting Pinetop to leave. He loved a good time and being around people. I hated to be the one to tell him we had to go. When I finally herded him out to the bus, much to my surprise Eric was aboard, sitting with Muddy. "I'm going with you," Eric joked. Muddy chimed in: "Yep, we're gonna take him with us." I told them it sounded good to me. Didn't happen, but I had to wonder if Eric wasn't half serious. I'm sure he would have enjoyed at least a short hop with Muddy and the band, just for the buzz of it.

```
MARCH 7 - 12, 1978          BRADFORD HOTEL            AMERICAN #476 [3/6/78]
                            275 Tremont
PAUL'S MALL                 Boston, Massachusetts 02116   Dpt. New York........9:45 am
733 Boylston Street         617/426-1400                  Arr. Boston.........10:35 am
Boston, Massachusetts 02116 1 Single
617/267-2051 or 267-1300
2/60 minute sets nightly
@ 8:30 pm & 11:00 pm
----------------------------------------------------------------------------------
MARCH 14 - 15, 1978                                      *****DRIVE*****

CREATION                          To Be Advised
414 Eagle Rock Avenue
West Orange, New Jersey 07052
201/731-3900                                             AMERICAN #277 [3/16/78]
1/75 minute set nightly @ 10:00 pm
SETUP: 4:00 pm                                           Dpt. Newark...........7:00 am
                                                         Arr. O'Hare...........8:12 am
----------------------------------------------------------------------------------
MARCH 17 - 18, 1978         SHERTON DOWNTOWN             DELTA #733 [3/17/78]
                            920 Broadway
EXIT INN                    Nashville, Tennessee 37203   Dpt. O'Hare...........2:05 pm
2208 Elliston Place         615/244-0150                 Arr. Nashville........3:13 pm
Nashville, Tennessee        6 Singles @ $22.00
615/327-2784                1 Double w/twin @ $27.00
2/60 minute shows nightly   RES# 015057140 & 015096778
@ 9:00 pm & 12:00 midnight
SETUP: 2:00 pm                                           DELTA #452 [3/19/78]

                                                         Dpt. Nashville........7:50 am
                                                         Arr. O'Hare...........9:04 am
```

Itinerary

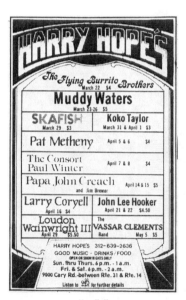

Handbill

Hawaii Festival poster

Eric Clapton Tour Europe 1978
(photo by Brian Bisesi)

Pinetop Perkins
(photo by Brian Bisesi)

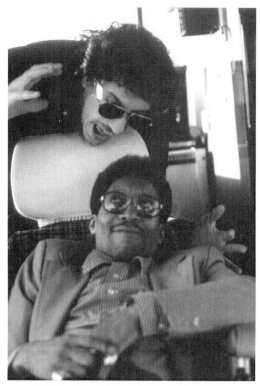

Bob Margolin and Willie Smith (photo by Brian Bisesi)

Pinetop on the bus (photo by Brian Bisesi)

Willie Smith at the wheel of the bus England 1978
(photo by Brian Bisesi)

Calvin Jones (photo by Brian Bisesi)

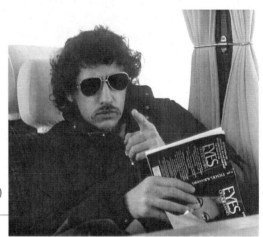

Bob Margolin
(photo by Brian Bisesi)

```
MUNICH JAZZ FESTIVAL 1979

July 17 - Tuesday

You take the special bus at hotel to go to the
OLYMPIA HALLE:                                  approximate
                                                performance time

     2. pm   SPYRO GYRA GROUP                      4.  pm
     3. pm   YOSUKE YAMASHITA TRIO                  4.50 pm
     4. pm   WOODY SHAW QUINTET                     5.40 pm .
     5. pm   SUPER JAM SESSION                      6.30 pm
             Al Grey, Jimmy Forrest,
             Sonny Stitt, Milt Jackson,
             Ray Bryant, Jimmy Woode,
             Duffy Jackson
5.30 6. pm   GROVER WASHINGTON                      7.20 pm
     7. pm   GEORGE SHEARING DUO / STEPHANE GRAPPELLI  8.25 pm
7.30 8. pm   LIONEL HAMPTON ALL STAR BAND           9.15 pm
     9. pm   B. B. KING BLUES BAND                  10.45 pm
    10. pm   DAVE BRUBECK QUARTET                   11.30 pm
    11. pm   MUDDY WATERS BLUES BAND                12.15 pm
             + JOHNNY WINTER
```

Munich Festival

Capital Jazz Festival, London, 1979 (photo by Patrick Hadfield)

Capital Jazz Festival, London, 1979 (photo by Patrick Hadfield)

Japan Tour Program

Pinetop and Guitar Junior
in Japan (photo by Brian Bisesi)

Pinetop Perkins (photo by Brian Bisesi)

Jerry Portnoy waiting on the train Tokyo, 1980
(photo by Brian Bisesi)

Willie Smith and the lion (photo by Brian Bisesi)

Guitar Junior in Japan (photo by Brian Bisesi)

Album cover Japan

Album cover Japan

Muddy puzzle

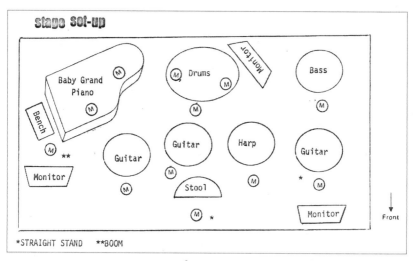

Stage set-up

MUDDY
WATERS

Muddy promo photo

Guitar case

Chapter 28

TAKE IT OR LEAVE IT

Our tour with Clapton was over, but Muddy had a few more dates in Europe before we headed back to the States, the first one being in London at the Rainbow Theatre on December 8. Then a day off in London, followed by a quick trip to Germany for a TV show called *Rockpalast*. From there it was back to London and another day off. The final show, on the twelfth, was also in London, a TV show called *The Old Grey Whistle Test*. That gig would fall apart at the last minute, which was kind of a relief. It gave us a day off, one we needed, before our return to the States.

As Muddy's contact person, in those final weeks overseas I got a call from the owner of a London club called Dingwalls. He was interested in having Muddy play there.

I told him that if it was going to happen, Dingwalls would have to make it really worthwhile for Muddy. That's our first day off in a while, I explained, the only one we have left before we fly. Muddy would probably rather rest than do a gig, I warned, but make a really good offer, and I'll bring it to him.

I forget the number Dingwalls's owner came up with, but it was low and I knew Muddy wouldn't go for it.

I took the bull by the horns. Look, I said. I can't even bring that offer to him. The owner repeated that he would really like to have Muddy play his club. How much would it take, he asked.

I didn't want to subject Muddy to the stress of a low-paying gig on a night he could be resting. But I also had a theory that I wanted to test. For the majority of the time that I worked for Muddy, I collected the money at the end of a gig, so I knew enough about the numbers. I knew how much his booking agent and manager settled for, and my hunch was that they could be getting a helluva lot more. Here was a chance to find out if I might be right.

I gave the Dingwalls owner a number: $3,000—more money than Muddy was getting from any club in the States at that time. The owner immediately blew me off. Look, he said, it's a small club. There's no way I can do that. I let him know again that I was not going to bring Muddy a lowball offer and we ended our conversation. A day later he called back, repeating how ardently he wanted Muddy to play Dingwalls. What would it take?

I said, okay, here's what we need: $3,000, to be paid in US currency, half paid in advance. Muddy will play for a specified length of time, and the other half of the money must be paid in cash—US dollars—before we leave the club. I wasn't trying to be difficult or a hard-ass, but I knew Muddy well enough to know what kind of deal he would agree to, if this was going to happen at all. I was borrowing a page from our tour manager Andy Zweck's playbook: Ask for it and the worst thing they can tell you is no.

Once again, the club owner started playing his violin, trying to break my heart. Dingwalls is a small club, he can't pay that kind of money, blah, blah blah. And I said once again that I wasn't going to bring Muddy a low number. After I hung up, I went to Muddy's room to tell him about the phone calls from a club in London. I told him the situation, that we had one day off that might work at the end of the tour, right after our return from Germany. I told Muddy about the $3,000 arrangement I presented to the club owner. Muddy's immediate reaction: "There's no way they'll go for that. No way."

Maybe not, I agreed, but if I can get that for you, will you do the gig? And he said, yes, hell yes, then repeated his conviction that there was no way they'd go that high. We agreed to just wait and see what happened. Within a day or two, I got another call from the Dingwalls owner. He capitulated. Totally. He said yes to the deal I had outlined. He wanted to make it happen. I went over the terms again and told him Muddy would expect the advance money to be delivered to the hotel immediately. Since our tour manager Andy Zweck had been

Eric Clapton, Muddy, me, and Willie Smith (clockwise from top left). Photo by Bob Margolin.

in charge of all monies on the Clapton tour, the club owner and I agreed that the money for the date could go through him. I reached Muddy in his room and told him we needed to talk. Muddy says: Talk about what? I told him I had just gotten off the phone with Dingwalls and that they had agreed to my price, the one Muddy said they'd never pay. "Whaaat!" he bellowed. He was thunderstruck. Now came the moment of truth, the big question. "Will you do it?" To my relief, he said yes again—assuming the advance money arrives as promised. I told him I'd let him know the minute it showed up. The deposit arrived and the only open date we had left was erased from our calendar.

Eric showed up at Dingwalls for the show, along with Pattie and Roger Forrester. The audience got more than they bargained for when Muddy called Eric to the stage to play a few songs with him.

The next day Muddy and I sat down together to pay the band for the club date. Muddy asked me how much I wanted for booking the gig. Normally Muddy's booking agent would get 10 percent and Scott Cameron, as Muddy's manager, would also get 10 percent. Since there was no booking agency involved, it came down to Scott's 10 percent, even though he had had nothing to do with the Dingwalls gig—didn't even know about it. It bothered me to think that Scott could tap into Muddy's take and get paid for doing nothing. What bothered me more was that if I—a twenty-three-year-old with limited experience as a road manager and no experience as a booking agent—could get more money for Muddy, then Scott and Muddy's booking agency should have been doing the same.

Muddy pressed me again about how much I wanted, and was startled by my answer: "Nothing. Just my regular pay for the night." Ten percent would be a nice piece of change, Muddy reminded me. I told him to spend it on his kids for Christmas. I didn't say this to Muddy, but I was hoping he wouldn't pay Scott his 10 percent. Later on he told me that he paid him anyway.

To my surprise Scott never said a word to me about booking that gig for Muddy, but he did seem to have a different attitude toward me after that. Muddy told me he had a talk with Scott about how I had been able to get more money for him in a club than he was used to, and after a while Muddy's price seemed to go up a bit. It made me feel good about what I had done in London. It seemed like my little experiment opened Muddy's eyes.

First footnote to the Dingwalls date: Ian Stewart, the Stones' pianist, got wind of it shortly before the show began. (I later found out he actually played the club the night before with Rolling Stones drummer Charlie Watts.) He wanted to know if it would be okay to make a recording, using the Stones' mobile studio. I told him he'd need Muddy's permission and suggested he ask him personally. "Who's this for?" Muddy wanted to know. Ian told Muddy it was for his personal entertainment. Muddy gave him the okay, as long as it was just for Stewart and the Rolling Stones' personal use. So, somewhere (I hope) in the Rolling Stones archives there may exist a recording of this particular night, Eric Clapton sitting in with Muddy in a relaxed club setting. And—hey, Mom!—I got to play, too! As I was standing by the stage with Forrester and Pattie Boyd, they unexpectedly pushed me up onto the bandstand. Muddy, as startled as I was by this development, turned to me, pointed to his guitar and told me to play it. So that would be me, playing Muddy Waters's guitar with Eric Clapton on "Got My Mojo Working."

A thrill indeed!

Second footnote: Earlier that evening, I tuned up the guitar Eric would be playing, the one he called "Blackie." And as I did so, he told me that it was put together from parts taken from various Stratocasters. So Blackie, it seems, was "a mutt" (that's how Eric referred to it). Eric forgot to take the guitar with him when he departed the club. He left it in the dressing room where I found it on my final check at the end of the night. As I was making my way out with the guitar slung over my shoulder in a gig bag, I bumped into a panicked Roger Forrester hauling ass down the hallway toward the dressing room. "Forgot something, Roger?" It was the only time I saw Roger with a panicked look on his face—totally out of character for him. I handed him the guitar and he thanked me profusely. I guess someone overcame the temptation to make off with one of the most legendary guitars in rock history!

Chapter 29

SWEET DREAMS

Life on tour had meant living in close quarters. Besides the endless hours on a bus (for this tour) and in airports, we sometimes needed to share rooms. To help me stay sane I established one rule: no eating on my bed. One evening I decided against enforcing it. Here's why.

It was our last night in London, and Eric and Pattie had stopped by the Holiday Inn to say goodbye to Muddy. For whatever reason, everybody decided to gather in the room I was sharing with Jerry Portnoy.

Eric and Muddy monopolized the only two chairs in the room and began talking shop. That left the beds for any of the rest of us who wanted to sit down. Pattie made herself comfortable on mine and promptly called room service to order some food. When it arrived, I answered the door and brought it over to her. She fluffed up a couple of pillows, leaned back and began to break my cardinal rule: no eating on the bed. It will come as no surprise that I decided against enforcing it. Or even mentioning it. After all, this was "Layla" breaking my rule! (Muddy also had some rules about his bed: no sitting on it (bad luck), and no women in the bed whose age added to his came to more than one hundred.

While Pattie munched, we had the blues for background music from a little cassette player. When William Brown's "Mississippi Blues" came on, Eric and Muddy stopped talking. Eric wanted to know who was singing. We told him it was Willie Brown, one of the pioneers of the Delta style along with Charlie Patton, Son House, and others. Eric asked if that was the Willie Brown that Robert Johnson mentions in his song "Crossroads" (". . . Tell my friend-boy Willie Brown"). Some of us piped in and innocently said that it was. That's what a lot of us thought in 1978, only to find out later that in fact we were listening to another Delta bluesman named William Brown. I guess someone figured out that Willie and William Brown had two completely different styles of playing so they had to be two different people. I will defer to the experts on that one. The recording we were listening to came from the Library of Congress. Bob Margolin turned me on to it after he got it from Johnny Winter. The amazing guitar playing had all of us mesmerized, but the song was still pretty obscure in 1978.

Muddy was clearly enjoying himself listening to blues and talking to Eric about the music he loved. And I'm sure for Eric it must have been a special moment to sit there talking with the legendary Muddy Waters about the equally legendary Robert Johnson. At the end of the night everybody was feeling pretty good. Muddy said his goodbyes to Eric and headed off to bed. Pattie and Eric got up to leave and gave Jerry and me hugs before they stepped into the elevator to go home. We would be flying back to the States in a few hours. It was time to get some sleep. As I reclaimed the bed Pattie had taken over, I caught Jerry Portnoy grinning at me. When I asked him what he was grinning about, he kind of laughed: "Well I guess you're going to have some sweet dreams tonight!" To which I replied: "I don't know if I'm going to be able to sleep at all tonight!"

Chapter 30

LIKE RIDING A BICYCLE

The next day we returned home and wouldn't work again until January 18, 1979—more than a month off. I learned from several members of the band that it was not unusual for Muddy to take a long break after Christmas. It was definitely a problem for many in the band: a long break with no money coming in and no retainer for their loyalty. They were expected to show up when it was time to reconvene regardless of how long the break was. In a way they felt slighted; Muddy had enough money to weather a long break—the band did not. This would eventually become another straw in the band's money dispute with Muddy and his manager Scott Cameron.

The first date once we were back on the road was in Tulsa, Oklahoma, a place called Cain's Ballroom. What I remember most about that gig was that when I took Muddy's guitar out of its case to tune it before the show, he told me he hadn't touched "that thing" since the last show some five weeks earlier. He seemed worried. I tried to put a positive spin on it and told him it was just like riding a bicycle: once you're on it, it all comes back to you. (Come to think of it, I'm not so sure Muddy ever rode a bike.) I told him not to worry, that he had been playing for so many years he would be fine. And he was. I had never seen a lack of confidence about anything with Muddy. This was the one time I did, and it really astonished me.

Whenever we had a few days off, the band (if possible) liked to go home, which for most of them meant Chicago. Better to have a few days at home than pay for a hotel room while you waited for the next gig. We started the 1979 touring with a three-day run, ending at the Palladium in Dallas on January 20. After some days off, the next gig would be at the Agora in Atlanta, January 26 and 27. It was winter and, true to form, most of the guys wanted to go back to Chicago for the off days. If I went with them that meant I would be helping with the driving and would have to pay for a hotel room since I had no one I could stay with in Chicago. Besides that, January in the Windy City is just too damn cold! I would prefer to spend the off days in Atlanta, if possible, where the winter is less severe. I got the impression that the guys in the band's idea of going from Texas to Atlanta was to head north to Chicago, stop for a day or two (at best), then drive southeast to Atlanta. Muddy asked me what my plans were. I told him I didn't want to go to Chicago, I would rather press on to Atlanta, visit some friends—and save on hotel costs.

That worked for Muddy. He told me that he didn't like the idea of both vehicles going back to Chicago and burning up gas that he was paying for. I offered to make my way east in one of the Suburbans. Phil Tripp, our Jazz Fest stage manager the previous year, was among my friends in Atlanta. He offered to put me up for the off days and to provide safe storage for the band's equipment. This sounded like a win-win to me. After a week at Phil's I could drive on to Charlottes-ville, Virginia, for our next show. Muddy told me to go ahead.

Now that the plan was set, the band loaded all of the amps into the vehicle that I was going to drive from Dallas to Atlanta, by way of Louisiana, Mississippi, and Alabama, about eight hundred miles. I initially thought if I got too tired I could pull off somewhere and get a room for the night. As I was driving along, only stopping in rest areas to refuel, reality hit me. I'm alone on the Interstate in the middle of nowhere and it's nighttime. My confidence was rapidly fading into fear. I had a vehicle full of equipment, and I didn't want to see the stuff get ripped off. If I left the vehicle unattended for too long, there was no telling what might happen. Getting a room for the night would mean unloading all the equipment and moving it into the room with me, then loading it back into the vehicle the next morning. Someone might see me doing this, and being alone I would be an easy target. Instead I decided to drive straight through to Atlanta. Upon arrival, Phil helped me move the equipment into his garage. Not the best arrangement, but at least it was secure. I stayed right through our Atlanta gig and spent the extra week visiting with friends while the band returned to Chicago (yet again). Now it was time to roll on to Charlottesville for a two-night engagement at the Mineshaft (February 7–8, 1979).

As I left Atlanta, it began to snow. Just a little dusting, I thought to myself, nothing to worry about. Wrong! The closer I got to South Carolina, the heavier the snow. This was turning into a major weather event. Transportation officials shut the Interstate down, but since I had most of the band's equipment with me, I had to make it to this gig. Being in a traveling band is often like being a mailman. Come rain, sleet or snow, you must deliver! By now there were very few vehicles left on the road, and I was proceeding at a crawl.

Finally, I made it to Virginia, and the band arrived from Chicago at about the same time—everyone except the star attraction. Muddy's flight had been canceled because of the storm, the one and only time Muddy missed a gig in the whole period I worked for him. He made it in time for the show the following night.

As Pinetop Perkins emerged from the Suburban from Chicago, he pointed at the front of the car I had been driving. I had no idea why. I knew I didn't hit anything on my trip. What caught Pinetop's eye was the six inches of ice coating the whole front of the Suburban. "Boy, how did you ever make it here?" Pinetop wanted to know. I told him that I drove r-e-a-l slow.

We didn't have cell phones in those days so you didn't always know what was going on between point A and point B. CB radios helped sometimes, but they couldn't tell you if a flight had been canceled or where the other guys were if I was traveling alone. We would often be traveling at night, pressed for time to make it to the next gig. We didn't always have access to flight information, or the ability to contact the club to give them a heads-up on our whereabouts. Or to find out if the gig was canceled while we were traveling through bad weather. A lot has changed since then. We have cell phones!

Chapter 31

RRRIIIIIPPPP

In March, we were in Boston for an engagement at the Paradise Rock Club (March 14–15, 1979). We had been on the move since the beginning of March on a series of dates that started in the Midwest and ran through upstate New York and into Canada before we hit Boston. Muddy flew home for days off, as usual. His clothes traveled with us in the back of one of the Suburbans. That way he could limit his luggage at the airport to a carry-on bag.

It was freezing cold when we arrived at the Travelodge in Brookline for a much-needed day off before we played the Paradise. All I could think of was sleep, which I did right through supper and into the night. The next morning I figured I would rest some more before Muddy blew in from the airport. The Travelodge we were staying in had parking slips in front of the rooms—a convenience when it came to unloading the Suburbans, but really cold in the wintertime whenever you opened the door to your room. I had Muddy's suitcase (which he called his "grip") in my room for safekeeping.

I was catching a few more winks before Muddy's arrival when suddenly I was jarred awake by someone pounding on my door. Oh, great, I'm thinking, a police knock. They're going to search my bags for pot. But no, it was Muddy, banging his meaty fist on the door so hard the whole room shook. Still comatose I made my way over to open the door, and Muddy came barreling in with a blast of frigid air at his heels. The door is still wide open when he starts in on a story: "You wouldn't believe what just happened to me!" So here I am half asleep, I've got one eye open and I'm looking at him and wondering what could possibly justify this rude awakening. As the story goes, he's getting into a cab at Logan Airport for the ride into Boston when he hears a sound. (Muddy mimics the sound of fabric ripping.) I noticed he has an overcoat on and a suit under that. I was not prepared for what came next.

He pulls the overcoat up over his waist and puts one leg up on the dresser. He says, "Look at this." His pants are split wide open, all the way through the crotch and halfway up his rear end. Dumbfounded, the only response I could conjure was, "Wow!" Thinking Muddy wanted to change his clothes, I offered to bring his suitcase to his room. Nope. Muddy had a higher priority. He was going to go down to the restaurant and get something to eat.

You don't want to change your pants first? He put his leg back down on the floor. "I'll just go into the restaurant and keep my overcoat on," he said, "slide into a booth and, once I'm sitting down, I'll take off my overcoat. Then after I finish eating, I'll put on my overcoat, and head on out. Pretty slick, huh?" I looked at him and he was laughing. "Yeah, pretty slick," I said. "You woke me up to tell me that?" He was still laughing. "Well, I had to tell somebody."

After Boston, we had another two weeks of dates in the Northeast before the long drive to Arizona to begin a tour (March 26, 1979) in Tucson with Eric Clapton that would last through the end of June.

Chapter 32

DEFINITELY A TRIPP

The Clapton tour brought us to New Orleans on April 15, 1979. Our venue was the Municipal Auditorium (across Rampart Street from the French Quarter, in Louis Armstrong Park). Our visit was not part of Jazz Fest that year, but coincided with it. Phil Tripp, my newfound friend from Atlanta, was working the festival again as a stage manager, and had come up with an excellent idea that also put a little money in his pocket. He rented an air-conditioned motorhome and parked it next to the stage he had been assigned. It offered respite from the New Orleans heat and doubled as a dressing room. Phil offered it for free to artists he liked. For artists who were, shall we say, a bit full of themselves, he imposed a small fee. Take your pick: wait for your set sweltering in the subtropical heat, or hang out in an air-conditioned living room. The motorhome was in heavy demand.

When we arrived in New Orleans, I got in touch with Phil. He offered to swing by our hotel in the motorhome, pick up Muddy and the band at the front door, and take us to the Municipal Auditorium, a short hop.

He wanted to surprise Muddy by having a chilled bottle of his favorite champagne waiting for him in the motorhome. I thought Muddy and the band would enjoy this so I gave Phil's plan a big thumbs-up. I promised to have everyone ready on time out front of the hotel on Rampart Street and not to tell Muddy about the surprise bottle of champagne that would be waiting for him.

Phil arrived on schedule and Muddy climbed into the motorhome and settled himself on the couch. The Piper-Heidsieck was in an ice bucket on the table in front of him, and Muddy was pleased, to say

Phil Tripp. Photo by Brian Bisesi.

the least. I opened the bottle and poured glasses for him and Pinetop Perkins. The two of them started talking about how great it would be to travel in a motorhome. Muddy was clearly enjoying himself. "Maybe I should get one of these," he said. Phil was at the wheel and just then he made a U-turn to loop around the Rampart Street median strip (or "neutral ground" as New Orleanians call their road dividers). Alas, to make the turn in a thirty-five-foot motor home meant that the wheels on the left side of the vehicle were going to bounce up onto the median strip's curb. The motorhome was rocking furiously as we negotiated the U-turn and Muddy's champagne was splattering all over the place. Muddy yelled out: "Tripp! What the hell are you doing up there?" Phil apologized for the rocky ride and Muddy sank back into his seat to enjoy the bubbly, then bellowed an afterthought: "Tripp, you know you got the right name, because you definitely is a trip!" We made it to the Municipal Auditorium without further incident, and the rocky "trip" to the venue in Phil Tripp's champagne-stocked motorhome became one of the stories Muddy loved to tell.

A week later, ahead of an evening show in Mobile, Alabama (April 22, 1979), I made my usual dry run to the venue that afternoon, to scope out the best route from the hotel and make sure we wouldn't get lost on our way to the show. Jerry Portnoy came along for the ride. In the venue's parking lot, we noticed a car driving around aimlessly. Jerry zeroed in on the person in the passenger seat, turned to me, and said, "That's Big Joe Williams."

Big Joe was a blues singer and songwriter known for his nine-string guitar and a career that spanned more than five decades. Big Joe first recorded "Baby Please Don't Go" for Lester Melrose's Bluebird label in 1935, a song Muddy played at almost every show. Big Joe had his driver pull over to where we were standing, and Jerry stepped to the passenger-side window. Big Joe was looking for Muddy, he said—just to say hello. When we told him Muddy wouldn't turn up until showtime that evening, Big Joe was disappointed. He was on his way to New Orleans to play the Jazz Fest and couldn't hang around all day.

He asked us to give Muddy his regards and to tell him he was sorry to miss him. But before he left, Big Joe found time to share some vintage memories of Muddy. One I had heard before: As a teenager Muddy played harmonica and Big Joe brought him around with him through the Delta for gigs at private parties, juke joints, and what have you. And then, abruptly, he decided to let Muddy go. Why? Because Muddy was taking all the women. Muddy had told me the story was true. The women were looking at him, not Big Joe, so, in Joe's mind, Mud needed to go. By the time I came on the scene in 1978, Muddy was in a long-term relationship with Sunshine, his third wife, and from what I saw, he was quite content and very happy with her, a woman about forty years younger than he was! Muddy still had an eye for pretty women, and he would often flirt with them playfully.

But in the time I spent traveling with him, I never saw Muddy indulge himself as the "womanizer" he was reputed to be. I'm not saying it didn't happen in his past, just not when I was around.

Then Big Joe told us another story about the trip he and Muddy and a whole group of the best blues artists made to Europe in 1963 for the famous American Folk Blues Festival: Sonny Boy Williamson II, Memphis Slim, Willie Dixon, Victoria Spivey, Lonnie Johnson, Otis Spann, and others. On the flight over, there had been a lot of turbulence. Muddy's acclaim had shot up with his many successful recordings, including "Got My Mojo Working" (Chess 1652, 1957) but he was still pretty new to flying, and the turbulence was freaking him out. Big Joe remembered Muddy coming over to him in kind of a dither: "Hey, Big Joe, I'm getting kind of scared here, tell me something to help me calm down." Big Joe could think of only one remedy: "Well, all I can tell you is if you gonna get that mojo working, you better get it working right now." I told that story to Muddy and he started laughing. He said, "Yeah, that's true. Big Joe didn't tell me anything that really helped, he just told me to get my mojo working."

We finished the first leg of the 1979 tour with Clapton on April 30, in Philadelphia at the Spectrum. The next leg wouldn't begin until May 25 in Augusta, Maine, more than three weeks later. Muddy decided to rest for the entire time.

So far, the tour had been absolutely wonderful—except for all the driving. I deeply missed the tour bus we had been provided on our European tour with Clapton.

For me this leg of the tour was also touched with sadness, and Muddy's reaction revealed how unpredictable he could be. One night in early June, I returned to the hotel after the show to find the light glowing on my phone: a message. It was from a friend. Call immediately. It was late, but he took my call. A very close friend of ours, a truck driver named Barry Jackson, had been killed that morning in a crash. I was devastated. Barry was engaged and I was to have been best man at the wedding, just a few weeks away. This was a guy I grew up with. He was a great drummer who just loved driving a truck and decided to put his sticks aside. I'm sure he could have made it in the music business, he was really that good.

Muddy had come to know Barry, a big fan of his who came as often as he could to Muddy's gigs in the New York area. Muddy had met Barry's fiancée, too. "Hey, I hear you're a good drummer," Muddy said to him one time. "Why don't you sit in?" Barry was a quiet, polite, reserved kind of guy. He would tell Muddy, "No, I'm here to see you." The morning after getting the bad news, I told Muddy what had happened and that I would have to miss our next show to go to the funeral because I'd been asked to be a pallbearer. Muddy looked at me and his reaction was unexpected: "Well, you can't help him now. You can't help him. He's already gone. You can't help him now."

"This is something I have to do," I replied. "I'm leaving today, to go back east. The funeral is in two days. You do whatever you have to do, I gotta do what I gotta do." So I flew back east, went to the funeral, and from there directly to the airport, still wearing my suit. I caught the first plane back to Chicago and the band picked me up at the airport. Everybody was very quiet when I arrived and not much was said. When we got to the venue that night in Madison, Wisconsin, I walked into the dressing room, wondering what Muddy was going to do—or if I even still had a job.

The first words out of his mouth: "Hey, come over here," and then, "Are you all right?" I told him I was very shaken by Barry's death. Muddy's next move took me by surprise. He reached into his pocket and pulled out my pay from the show I had missed. "Here's your pay from last night," he said. "I want you to take it." I said, "No, that's all right." Muddy insisted, "I want you to take it, and I'm very sorry about what happened to your friend." The point, I guess, is that Muddy could really be a mixed bag. He could come out with a very hurtful comment and then, seconds later, could be caring and fatherly. He let you know that he felt for you and was there for you.

Chapter 33

ERIC, MEET JOHNNY

That was the low point of the Clapton tour for me. One of the best nights came about a week later. It was at Chicago Stadium (June 12, 1978), then still the home court for pro basketball's Chicago Bulls. That meant Muddy was performing for his hometown crowd. Johnny Winter came in that night and surprised Muddy. Willie Dixon was there, too. Muddy was really happy to see them and, naturally, called both up onto the stage to sit in. Winter was hanging out in the dressing room with Muddy before the show. At one point I stepped out to attend to some detail and, returning to the dressing room, figured it would be a good time to use the men's room.

I was at the sink washing up when Winter came out of one of the stalls and took his place at the sink next to mine. I said to Johnny, you and Eric must be old friends. You guys must have known each other through the years, so this is great, having both of you here with Muddy. Winter turned to me and said, "I've never met Eric Clapton." I figured he was kidding. "No, I've never met him." I was kind of amazed: "Out of all the years that you guys have been out there traveling and playing, you never once crossed paths?" And he said, "I never met him, I'd like to meet him."

I said, "Johnny, come with me." I brought him to Eric's dressing room, which was a short distance away. I was thinking to myself, this is going to be good. I knocked on the door and someone cracked it open. I could see Eric sitting there with Forrester, his manager. "I have Johnny Winter here to see Eric," I announced loudly, and the door opened wide enough to let us in. Eric rose from his seat, a big smile on his face, and Johnny was smiling, too.

Eric Clapton, Muddy Waters, and Johnny Winter (Chicago Stadium, June 12, 1979).
Photo by Paul Natkin. Wirelmage/Getty Images.

I did the introductions: "Johnny, Eric Clapton. Eric, Johnny Winter."
Then I got out of the way. "I'm sure you two have a lot to talk about."
As I left the room, I saw them sit down together and immediately
dive into conversation—a wonderful moment that I was very happy
to have engineered. It blew my mind that they had never met before.
The two of them went on to become friends and Johnny wound up
playing on some of Eric's Crossroads Guitar Festivals many years later.
There are some great pictures from that night at the Chicago Stadium:
Willie Dixon, Johnny Winter, and Eric Clapton on stage with Muddy.
Dixon had been the first to be called onto the stage. Then Muddy hol-
lered for "my son Johnny Winter" and "my other son Eric Clapton."

It was a great moment—for the three guest musicians, not to mention the stadium audience. Needless to say it was special for me too,
the night I got to introduce Johnny Winter to Eric Clapton!

While we toured America with Clapton, he based operations out
of Chicago for a while. With a plane chartered for the tour, he could
fly from Chicago to nearby venues in Wisconsin, Michigan, and Minnesota and not have to constantly change hotels, or unpack and repack
his luggage.

Cars weren't Muddy's only vehicular passion. One time he got me to take him from his house to Midway Airport in Chicago and fly with him on Eric's plane. We were pleased to learn that we could park Muddy's Lincoln, the Big Yellow Cat, right next to the plane.

During that flight with Clapton, Eric tried to play card tricks on me. I had brought a cassette tape with me of the Fabulous Thunderbirds first album (Takoma 7058, 1979). The Thunderbirds were not yet widely known, and I think it was one of the first times Eric had really heard them. We played it on the plane's tape recorder as we flew. Muddy was a big fan of the Thunderbirds. They opened many shows for him at Antone's, in Austin. Muddy thought highly of Kim Wilson's singing and harmonica playing along with Jimmie Vaughan's top-notch guitar style.

Chapter 34

A NIGHT ON THE TOWN

Ahead of a welcome night off, Eric's manager Roger Forrester contacted me. Eric wanted to check out the blues scene in Chicago. Could I take him to a couple of clubs with live music? I said sure. (So much for my night off.)

Forrester added that he didn't want to be reading about Eric's night on the town in the papers the next day. I got it. This was to be a low-key evening. For starters we'd have to dodge the photographers hanging around the hotel trying to get pictures of Eric and Pattie. Luck was with us. The paparazzi were off duty. Albert Lee, a guitarist with Clapton's band, came down from their rooms with Eric and Pattie and we escaped the lobby without triggering the usual explosion of flashbulbs.

I flagged down a cab and took them over to the North Side where there were few good clubs within a couple of blocks of each other. Eddie Taylor was playing at a place called B.L.U.E.S. on Halsted. A club called the Kingston Mines was a walkable few blocks away. If everyone wanted more music, we could go on to the Wise Fools Pub, also within walking distance, I told them. My plan fell apart rather quickly.

At B.L.U.E.S., our first stop, I managed to get us a table right in front of where Eddie Taylor was playing, and we settled in without anybody pestering the superstars in their midst. Eric had come prepared with a flask of brandy and only needed a glass and some 7-Up, which he called lemonade. The waitress didn't seem to notice a customer bringing booze into the club to spike the soda pop he'd paid for, and if anybody even recognized Eric and Pattie, they were cool about it.

As we sat there admiring Eddie's brilliant guitar work—Eric's first time hearing him live—I noticed the ceiling had a tiny leak and that water was dripping right onto Eric's head. I offered to move us over to a dry table. "No, I don't want to move," he said. "This is like watching Picasso paint." Taylor was a masterful artist who made many great records with Jimmy Reed and other blues geniuses. (Later on I got to know him a little bit and played with him a few times myself.)

When the set was over, Eric got up and exchanged a few words with Taylor. Eric was polite and deferential and I doubt Taylor had a clue who was talking to him. But folks in the audience were bound to recognize the Brit and so I figured it was time to move on to another club. I suggested the Kingston Mines and everyone seemed okay with just walking there.

I knew some of the people who worked at the Mines. They let us in, no problem, and seated us at a little table off in a quiet corner. Eddy Clearwater, another great guitarist and master of the Chicago style, was playing that night. As we settled in, one of the waitresses I knew came over to give me a heads-up. The club owner had just called a photographer, a good friend of mine, as it happened. The club's front window was plastered with pictures of rock stars—Rolling Stones, Allman Brothers, and more—who had paid a call on the Mines. The club owner badly wanted to add Eric's picture to his collection.

I had to think fast. To complicate matters, Eric was starting to get pretty loaded. Albert Lee decided that he wanted to split. I went outside with him to hail a cab so he could return to the hotel. Back inside, as soon as I sat down, Pattie turned to me and asked for a cab.

She could see that things were beginning to take a turn for the worse and was ready to call it a night. Not Eric. I came back from escorting Pattie into a cab and found him standing prominently by the stage talking to Eddy Clearwater, who had invited him to sit in.

With the photographer already on his way, I wanted to make sure Eric wasn't up on stage when he arrived. A photo in tomorrow's papers would violate my vow to Forrester to keep Eric's club hopping on the down low. Yes, Mission Control, we had a problem. I had to get Eric out of there in a hurry. So, I just came out with it. "Eric, we've got to go." He looked at me blankly. "No," he said, "I'm going to play with Eddy Clearwater." I told him we really had to go because I had promised Roger that there wouldn't be any photo of our night on the town. There's a photographer on his way over here right now, and I don't want to get into it with Roger. "Eric, we gotta go," I said. To which Eric responded: "Fuck you."

He was pretty drunk by then, so I tried appealing to his better nature. "I know you didn't mean that," I said, "so let's try it again: We gotta go." Again he said, "Fuck you." And then he raised his fist and hit me lightly across the chin. Kind of a playful punch, but now we really had a situation going on. "I don't want to get into it with you," I said. I was a young guy in pretty good shape and with a truckload of Jersey attitude. I was in no mood for this kind of bullshit. So I told Eric, "You've got two choices. Either you walk out of here with me or I'm going to drag your ass out of here, which one you wanna do?" Again he says, "Fuck you." "Okay," I said, "then I'm going to have to drag your ass out of here." He looked at me and kind of smiled then he put his arm around me and said, "All right, let's go." I got him into a cab and took him back to his hotel. And that was the end of that.

My friend the photographer didn't get the picture he wanted but never made an issue of it with me. He understood the whole situation and we remained good friends. I hated to be in that mess with Eric because I had so much respect for him, and on most occasions he was sociable and fun to be around. The plan was for a nice night out and then things went south fast, so I had to get him out of there. My reward: I guess I'm an honorary member of the club that Eric Clapton said "fuck you" to.

Chapter 35

FOR THE BYRDS

In due course, the tour brought us to Nebraska and the Omaha Civic Auditorium (June 18, 1979). I had played this venue with Muddy the year before when I was filling in for Guitar Junior. I remembered the gig for two reasons. It was the first time I played in front of a large crowd and we opened for Sha Na Na, an odd pairing.

At the show that night with Clapton, I noticed someone walking around the stage area with a walkie talkie. He looked an awful lot like Roger McGuinn from the Byrds, but I figured it must be a security guy. I mean what would Roger McGuinn be doing at an Eric Clapton/ Muddy Waters show with a walkie talkie in hand? I would find out about McGuinn, if not the walkie talkie, a few hours later.

I was in my hotel room later that night, getting ready for bed when someone knocked on my door. At this hour? I made my way over to the peephole and to my surprise it was Clapton. What could he possibly want and how did he even find me? This was probably the only time we stayed in the same hotel during the two tours we did with Eric. I opened the door to let him in.

He needed my help, he said. He was at a card game in the hotel with the Byrds and he thought they were cheating. Eric asked me to join him in the card game because he wanted someone he could trust that he knew wouldn't be cheating. I was flattered that he viewed me as someone he could trust, but I couldn't afford to lose money in a card game with a bunch of cheating Byrds.

I told Eric my situation. Don't worry about the money, he replied. He said he'd give me enough to play. I still felt uncomfortable about the possibility—probability—of losing Eric's money. I told him, no, I couldn't do it. But I knew someone I could call who would probably love to join the card game: Fuzz!

Calvin Jones would often ask me to take him to Atlantic City, if we were ever in the area—Atlantic City, in my home state, being one of the few places outside Nevada that had legal gambling at the time. I never did get to take him there, but a card game in the hotel might work. I reached Fuzz in his room. I told him what was up and that Eric needed someone to go with him. Fuzz was dressed and in my room in less than five minutes.

After some small talk and a shot of Hennessy, Eric, and Fuzz departed for the card game, or so they thought. The next morning as I was loading my bags into one of the Suburbans, Fuzz was doing the same. I was curious to hear how the card game went. Fuzz told me they never found out where the game was being played because the guys kept moving it to different rooms. Instead, he and Eric wandered around the hotel for a while before packing it in. I had wanted to help Eric when he asked me to go to the card game with him and I have to admit it would have made an interesting story—gambling with Eric Clapton and the Byrds. But I was glad they never found the game because Fuzz definitely didn't need to be losing any money. We weren't making that much to begin with.

Our next stop was Wichita, Kansas, about a three-hundred-mile drive, not too bad, I thought. I would soon learn how wrong I was.

About two hundred miles into the trip it was time to refuel. I was in the lead vehicle with Willie, Pinetop and Jerry. The drive had been uneventful so far, just another day on the road. All of that changed when we pulled in for gas at a Kansas station. It was midafternoon, but darkness was already setting in. As we finished refueling the two vehicles, the gas station attendant told us why. There were tornados in the area. Be careful, he warned us.

We had seen plenty of bad weather in our travels and always made it to the gig. Besides the attendant said the threat was "possible tornados," not a full-tilt warning. I kept looking at the sky. It was turning a color I had never seen before, and it was getting darker, much darker. Suddenly the wind kicked up and it started pouring rain, pouring so hard the windshield wipers were of no use. Fortunately, this happened just as we were approaching an underpass. Willie pulled over to the side of the road figuring we could just wait there until the rain let up. It was now totally dark and the downpour had reduced visibility to zero. The vehicle began rocking side to side and I wondered if we might tip over.

Willie turned on the interior lights and Pinetop Perkins leaned over the seat to tell us a story about the time he was in Mississippi on the farm when a tornado hit. He described how, as he watched, the storm lifted a cow into the air, never to be seen again. Not exactly comforting words to hear just then. If a tornado could do that to a cow it should have no problem tipping this vehicle over, I thought to myself.

Fortunately, we didn't tip over and the storm blew by after what seemed like forever but was probably only a few minutes. With the sky beginning to clear again we pushed on to Wichita—only to find out the tornado threat had shuttered the airport in Omaha. Eric and Muddy couldn't fly to Wichita. Gig canceled!

To make matters worse, Kansas was a dry state. After the kind of day we had just been through, I could use a drink to calm my nerves. Fortunately, at the restaurant that night I was able to get one, thanks to some bizarre state law that allowed you a drink if you agreed to pay a one-time "membership fee." I had to laugh as I sipped my drink and remembered the words of wisdom (warning) that Victoria Spivey told me the first time I met her. "Anyone who wants to be a musician has got to be half crazy to begin with. By the time you become one you're completely crazy because of all the changes you will go through."

We had three dates left on the tour; the next one was in Salt Lake, a fourteen-hour drive, then on to Washington, with gigs in Spokane and Seattle (June 24). I dreaded what would come next: a nonstop, two-thousand-mile drive back to Chicago. Forty hours on the road. I had done it with the band the previous year. Like the year before, Bob and Jerry wanted no part of it, so they flew back east. Smart move. We arrived in Chicago and had barely enough time to catch our breath. There were still two shows scheduled, the first one in New

Victoria Spivey and me, Brooklyn, New York, 1976. Photo by Ralph Bisesi.

York City (June 29) for the 1979 Newport Jazz Festival: "A Tribute to Muddy Waters," featuring B.B. King, James Cotton, and Johnny Winter. Muddy, still riding high from the Clapton tour we just finished, was thrilled and honored to be with his dear friends that night. The next day it was onward to Saratoga, New York, before some badly needed time off, three days' worth. Next up, a seventeen-day trip to Europe for some festivals. The good news: we wouldn't have to drive!

We returned to the States from London on July 23 for a much-needed week off. August 3 found us back in the Windy City at the Navy Pier for ChicagoFest. What I remember most about this show was that when I went to retrieve Muddy's guitar from his car it wasn't there. After some initial panic, Muddy realized that Bo (Andrew Bolton) forgot to put "Hoss" in the trunk before Muddy left home that day. After Muddy's initial reaction—"Oh, shit! What am I gonna do?"—I offered to let him play my guitar, which was in my hotel room a few blocks away along with a capo, which I knew he would want as well. Muddy was all in on the idea and told me to get moving—fast! And indeed, I hauled ass, running on foot from the Navy Pier back to my hotel room. I recently saw a photo of Muddy playing that guitar, a 1959 Fender Stratocaster. Funny thing is, when he played it, he sounded like Muddy. When I played it, I didn't!

After that festival, there wasn't much on the schedule until September 11, a festival in Toronto at the Ontario Place Forum. The following day: a one-nighter in East Syracuse, New York. Things were starting to change. Usually the big "off period" was around Christmas, now there was one for most of August and the beginning of September. The seeds were planted; money—or, shall we say, the lack of it due to less work—was going to become a shaping factor, an ugly one, in our not-too-distant future. But first, a respite: Things picked up again in late September and into October. The final three dates in October (26–28) were at one of Muddy's "home" venues, Harry Hopes in Cary, Illinois.

We had a couple of days off in Chicago before flying to Mexico City for a festival (November 1–4, 1979) with Willie Dixon, Blind John Davis, Son Seals, and Koko Taylor. The day before our arrival, a Western Airlines flight from Los Angeles had crashed on the runway in Mexico City, killing seventy-two of the eighty-eight passengers on board. The wreckage was still visible as we landed, a sad reminder of how fragile life on the road can be.

Since Mexico City was new to most if not all of us, we had no idea of how the festival audience might react to some of Chicago's finest blues. They went nuts! At each of the sold-out shows the crowd roared with approval for all of the acts. A few of the musicians, Pinetop Perkins among them, donned sombreros, to everyone's amusement.

After the opening night, some of us gathered the next morning in Willie Smith's room back at the hotel. A lack of weed was the concern. After a brief discussion, one member of Koko Taylor's band volunteered to hit the streets in search of the desired herb. We figured a guy with no Spanish on the streets in a foreign land would have zero chance of scoring. Ten minutes later, a knock on the door. Cops? No,

Mexico City Festival poster.

in comes Koko's bass player with a paper bag chock full of weed. Where did he find it? Next door to the hotel, the parking-lot attendant sold him the bag for $5.

"Okay, let's split this shit up, everybody owes me $1.25," he announced. The guys were thinking more like a few joints to get through the few days we had in Mexico. Oh, well, I guess it's either feast or famine.

The festival organizers offered to transport anyone playing the festival to the ancient pyramids in Teotihuacan, about thirty miles from Mexico City. Muddy, and pretty much everyone else, had no interest in seeing this historic site. But Koko Taylor wanted to have a look, so off we went. When we arrived, some of us decided to climb the bigger of the two pyramids, the Pyramid of the Sun, one of the largest pyramids on the planet. Koko wanted no part of that, no way. Looking was enough for her.

The Mexico trip was great, but we all looked forward to going home for a few days before the next tour cranked up, on November 9 in New York City. Unfortunately, when we arrived at the airport, we found out that many flights had been canceled, including some of ours. I believe the problem was the airport had only one runway open. Since the fatal crash a few days earlier, they weren't taking any chances. Finally, after some major juggling, I managed to get everyone on a flight. That is, everyone except me. I definitely did not want to be stranded in Mexico. I pleaded with the ticket agent to get me on any flight bound for the United States. After hearing *"no es posible"* several times, I secured a flight to Dallas. I would find my way back to the New York area from there.

Muddy did three shows, November 9, 10, and 11, 1979, with B.B. King and Bobby Bland, a triple treat for blues lovers. The first was in New York at the Beacon Theatre, followed by Symphony Hall in Newark, New Jersey, followed by Shea's Theatre in Buffalo, New York. Newark and Buffalo were interesting because the audiences were predominantly Black and, when a lyric moved them, they responded to the music more vocally than whiter audiences. To me it like was being in the Gospel Tent at the New Orleans Jazz Fest. By contrast, the crowd at the Beacon would applaud politely at the end of a song. And everyone at the Newark and Buffalo shows were dressed in their Sunday best. Bobby Bland drew the biggest buzz from the ladies, and any semblance of church-like decorum gave way. Dozens of them rushed to the edge of the stage and tossed handkerchiefs to him to wipe the sweat from his brow, then shrieked ecstatically when he handed the damp hankies back to a lucky few. There may have also been a couple of intimate articles thrown up there, too.

At the end of the night, B.B. King and Muddy were unwinding in the dressing room when B.B. offered Muddy a ride in his limo back to the hotel. I was astounded when Muddy turned to me and said

I could come with them. Riding in a limo with Muddy Waters and B.B. King? Never in my wildest dreams could I have imagined that!

There were about a half-dozen dates left before Muddy took his extended annual break from touring. This time it would extend from December 9 through January 18, 1980. This is the period when some of the guys formed the Legendary Blues Band. Muddy had been accepting less work for the previous six months, and that had taken a toll on everyone's bank account. Bob Margolin had been working around the Washington, DC, area during periods when Muddy wasn't performing, so he was able to get through the lean times okay. Same for Guitar Junior; he was able to find work on the West Side in Chicago. The rest of the guys felt confident there were more lucrative paydays outside of Chicago, in places like Boston, Washington, DC, and upstate New York. Some dates were booked for early January. Jerry Portnoy pulled most of it together, though I can claim credit for booking a DC date. I was grateful to play guitar with them for the few dates they had; I needed the money, too.

Muddy got wind of all this when Willie Smith called him, explained the money problem the band faced, and asked Muddy if he could use one of the vehicles, the one that always stayed with Willie whether we were on the road or not. Muddy's answer deeply hurt Willie: "No." With no transportation, and some dates already booked, a plan B was needed. Calvin Fuzz Jones offered up his recently acquired, used but beautiful Cadillac El Dorado. The plan was to hitch a U-Haul trailer onto the back of the Caddy for the equipment. We made all of the dates, and I think it gave the guys a lot of confidence in case they had to do this again in the future. And they did. When we met up with Muddy again on January 18, in Tulsa, the first thing he wanted to know: "How much you make?" The only answer he got was "we did all right."

Fortunately, starting in February 1980, our schedule was looking good thanks to Rosebud, the San Francisco–based booking agency. Everyone in the band was happy, and there was no talk of more dates

CAMERON

DATE: March 6, 1980

TO: Brian Bisesi
                 Luther Johnson
                 Calvin Jones
                 Bob Margolin
                 Pinetop Perkins
                 Jerry Portnoy
                 Willie Smith

FROM: Scott Cameron

SUBJECT: Morganfield, Inc.
                 Independent Contractor Fees

- - - - - - - - - - - - - - - - - -

Muddy is pleased that beginning with this engagement,
March 6, 1980 Chicago, Illinois, the amount of the
Independent Contractor Fees paid for your services
rendered to Morganfield, Inc. has been increased as
follows:

	Old Fee	New Fee
One night	130.00	150.00
Two nights same location	180.00	200.00
Three nights same location	190.00	220.00

While doubtful, should an engagement (excluding foreign)
be scheduled four to seven days same location, the old
fee was 250.00, the new fee would be 280.00.

We hope that this increase will be beneficial to you.
Additional monies for driver's fees and/or requested
individual deductions are not reflected above.

Thank you !

PERSONAL MANAGEMENT
THE CAMERON ORGANISATION, INC.
320 South Walola Avenue, La Grange, Illinois 60525 (312) 352-2026

New pay scale, March 1980.

for the Legendary Blues Band. There was no need. I noticed with
the new agency Muddy's fees were increasing, too. I was happy that
things seemed to be moving in the right direction at last. I had always
believed Muddy was being booked too cheap. He was now getting
$4,500 to $5,000 for a concert date. It was long overdue.

The sailing got a little less smooth in early March. Scott Cameron presented the band with a memo, on March 6 to be precise, outlining a new pay scale for what were declared to be "independent contractor fees." It basically amounted to a $20 per gig increase. That was fine for a one-nighter, the old pay was $130. The new "fee" was $150. It was the two- and three-night gigs where things got problematic. The new amount was $200 for two nights, $220 for three. Anyone could do the math: The pay for a two-night gig had shrunk to $100 a night; for three nights, to $73.33. The expenses (hotel, food, etc.) stayed the same regardless of how long the engagement lasted. This was a major problem for the band. Over the past few years, "stagflation" had goosed hotel and food costs to unprecedented highs. Each of us was responsible for those expenses, plus income tax, which was not deducted from the nightly pay. Forget about health insurance; no one could afford it.

The band had no say in the new contractor fees. It was basically a take-it-or-leave-it deal. The band's anger was directed at Cameron, not Muddy. Although they knew it was ultimately Muddy's decision to go along with it or come up with something better. Everyone realized Scott had great influence over Muddy, and he viewed the band as hired guns, nothing more. Loyalty didn't matter; the sound that Muddy had cultivated and then grown accustomed to—a seven-year musical achievement—wasn't taken into consideration either. In conversations on more than one occasion, Scott saw fit to remind me (and by extension the band members), "Independent contractors can be easily replaced." I wasn't so sure about that one. We were barely three months into what we thought was going to be a promising year and then this happens. Things quickly got much worse.

PART THREE

Chapter 36

BUMPED FOR JOHNNY

Muddy and his generation of players, the older guys, were very proud of the fact that they had come up from nothing and that the blues had changed their lives forever. Their music was something that people wanted to hear all around the world. It brought them respect, which was in short supply in the agrarian South, where they came from, and in the urban north (Chicago, in particular) where they infused the blues with the force and popularity of rock.

But all the older bluesmen that I was ever around, Muddy included, shared a concern about the future of the music. It was important to them that the blues stay alive. They were afraid that no one was going to carry on their tradition. They looked to the younger players—many of us white guys—to keep the blues alive.

Muddy had a mantra: "Keep this thing going, don't let it die." He said it to bluesmen young and old, white and Black. I remember one time being backstage at a club with Kim Wilson from the Fabulous Thunderbirds. The two of us were sitting alone with Muddy. Muddy was about to go on stage when he turned to us and said, "You guys got to carry it on, don't let it die. Keep this thing going." We knew he was referring to the music. With Muddy gone, Kim turned to me: "Did you hear that? Did you hear what he just said to us? That's really heavy." We both understood this was a passing of the torch. Not that there weren't great bluesmen to carry the music along until we, the next generation, were ready to take the helm. Some of the financial constraints were because of cutbacks in the amount of work Muddy could accept, given health issues. His health was something Muddy did not usually talk about, but I knew he had mentioned it to some of the guys in the band.

Tension about the new pay scale continued to dog the band. The hurt and disappointment were still there, but they went out every night anyway and played their best behind Muddy. A lot of times when Muddy didn't feel up to doing an encore, let alone a second encore, he would have Guitar Junior do it instead. And in that same spirit, Bob Margolin would sometimes hand me his guitar and I'd back Junior and do the encore in Bob's place. As often as not, Junior's choice for the encore would be "I'm a King Bee," the song written and originally recorded by swamp bluesman Slim Harpo (Excello Records, 1957). Muddy really liked that song, he loved the way Junior sang it, and he complimented me on the way I accompanied him. When he told me he was going to record "I'm a King Bee," I asked if I could do it with him, he thought for a minute, then said, "Yeah, I like the way you played that. Okay, you got it."

King Bee would turn out to be Muddy's last album. Johnny Winter was going to produce it, at a studio in Westport, Connecticut. By early May we were in the Westport studio, The Schoolhouse. For most of the session, I sat in front of Muddy, holding up the lyrics to new songs that he wasn't familiar with. "Be careful not to rattle the paper," Muddy cautioned. "The vocal mike will pick it up." The new songs were material written by Muddy. One exception was "No Escape from the Blues," by his stepson Charles Williams. I was thrilled to be at ringside as musical history was being made, a Muddy Waters recording session. Unfortunately, Muddy's heart didn't seem to be in it. He rushed through one take after another on some of the songs, resulting in sessions that yielded slim pickings.

I had had a conversation with Muddy a few weeks before the session, and we had talked about the possibility of his playing one song on his old Gretsch guitar, without accompaniment. The reason this came up was because one time when I was at Muddy's house in Westmont, I asked him whatever happened to the guitar he used on "I Can't Be Satisfied" (Aristocrat 1305, 1948). I was floored when he told me he still had it, and that it was in a closet down the hall, a Gretsch Synchromatic. I asked if I could see it. No such luck. He said it was in bad shape. Just before the recording session, I mentioned again the idea of his doing a song by himself on that old guitar that launched his career. For a moment he seemed game, but wondered if people would really want to hear something like that. I assured him that fans would LOVE it, especially on that ancient guitar. Muddy asked me if I knew anyone who could fix it and where he might get the DeArmond pickup he needed for it. I told him I did, but the idea lost ground to other preoccupations and, to my lasting regret, we never went any further with it.

Johnny Winter did double duty on the session, playing and producing. The control room was upstairs, so when there was a song he wanted to play on, he'd bound down the steps and grab his ever-ready Gibson Firebird. In between songs he would communicate with Muddy from the control room, and we'd hear his comments through monitors set up in the studio. After each song Johnny would ask Muddy what he was going to do next. Finally, Muddy told me that the moment had come to record "I'm a King Bee." I was making my way over to where the band was set up—thrilled, of course, to be included on the recording—when Johnny comes running down the stairs from the control room, tells Muddy he loves that song and is going to play on it. I went from up, up, up to down, down, down faster than an elevator in a New York City skyscraper. Muddy gave me a really apologetic look. "I'm sorry," he said. "I know I said that you could play on this one, but Johnny wants to play and I gotta go with it." I told Muddy I understood. I was crushed but I understood. I got bumped for Johnny Winter. I can live with that!

Chapter 37

SABOTAGE?

Somewhere along the way, Muddy must have talked with Eric Clapton about the *King Bee* recording session and, according to what Scott Cameron told me, Eric wanted to play on it, too. Muddy was happy to have him, you can be sure. Or, with the wisdom of hindsight, let me put it this way: Muddy would have been happy to have him.

For Eric it was going to mean catching the supersonic Concorde from London to New York's Kennedy Airport. Cameron called to suggest that I pick Eric up at JFK and drive him to the studio in Westport. I said I'd be happy to play chauffeur, but that I wanted to figure out the logistics. "I'll get back to you," I said to Cameron. I figured Eric would be arriving with luggage and a flight case for his guitar, "Blackie." I wanted to think through all the possible scenarios that could unfold at the airport so that there would be no snags. I also didn't know if Eric would be traveling alone or with Pattie, by then his wife.

The more I thought about it, the more what-ifs came up. What if the luggage and road case don't fit in my car? What if I can't find a parking spot near the Concorde terminal? Kennedy has a lot of traffic and parking is not easy. Could one person pull this off? Park my car, go into the terminal to meet Eric, collect his luggage, and make it back to my car without him being noticed or me being ticketed. I was also concerned about what shape he would be in when he reached in New York, given the bar service on the plane. Perhaps if I could get someone to accompany me. . . .

I made a few exploratory calls to friends to see if I could drum up a van or a second car and driver. Then it dawned on me that we should call Blue Sky Records. Muddy and Johnny playing with Eric Clapton?

I was sure they'd be more than willing to arrange for a car to pick up Eric and drive him to the studio. To me, this was the workable plan. I would meet Eric at the International Arrivals building, help him with his luggage, and bring him to a car waiting outside. In those days you could have a car idling out front of the terminal (especially if it was a limo with a chauffeur). Nowadays, they'd chase you away. So, I called Cameron to discuss the details with him. I told him I had given this a lot of thought. "I'd love to pick Eric up at the airport," I told him, "but here's my problem. I've got a Buick and it doesn't have a very big trunk. As far as I know, Eric is going to be carrying his guitar in its flight case and it might be too big."

That was not the biggest problem; I'd figure out a way to fit in the guitar even if I had to tie the trunk down. The bigger problem was going to be parking. The parking garage is a considerable distance from the terminal at JFK. I would need to go inside to meet Eric as he came through customs, and then collect his luggage. What do I do with Eric while I go get my car? I knew from being around him on two tours that I didn't want to be responsible if he wandered off while I was retrieving my car. I doubted he'd have crossed the Atlantic without a drink or two or three, and I didn't know what kind of situation he might get himself into.

So, I pleaded my case to Scott. I said I was confident that if he told Blue Sky Records that Eric Clapton was flying in from England to play on a Muddy Waters record produced by Johnny Winter, they'd be more than happy to send a limo. I could still meet Eric at the airport to help him with his guitar and luggage and accompany him to the studio in Westport.

No dice.

Scott, for reasons I couldn't fathom at the time, was unwilling to call and request the car. Only later did I begin to see a pattern in Cameron's behavior, one that doomed not just the record but the last phase of Muddy's storied career as a touring bluesman. Scott, I came to see, was more and more concerned about his job, his role as Muddy's manager, and about maintaining control. In my view, he felt very threatened by Eric's manager, Roger Forrester, and by

Muddy's deepening relationship with Eric. Muddy really loved Eric, truly thought of him as a son. Muddy was thrilled and grateful to have done two tours with Eric. He was keenly aware of how opening for Eric in sold-out arenas had expanded Muddy's fan base. Eric's manager made that happen, not Cameron. In a moment of candor, Muddy had told me he knew Scott couldn't take him to the next level, whereas Roger could. Muddy and I had several conversations about it. I'm sure even Scott was aware of his limitations as a manager. And yet, regardless of those shortcomings, Muddy remained loyal to him.

There was more to it than just stubbornness about calling the record label for a car. It dawned on me later on that Scott seemed to be playing a deeper control game. It wasn't just that he didn't seem to want Eric on the album. If he had his way, he'd probably chase him right out of Muddy's professional life. In my opinion, Scott was that worried. Maybe he feared that eventually the Clapton connection might cost him his job.

Further evidence in support of my hunch had come a few months earlier in November 1979. One afternoon around Thanksgiving I had been at my parents' house in New Jersey when Forrester called. How Eric's manager tracked me down remains a mystery. He wanted to talk about a fresh possibility: a possible tour of Japan, with us opening for Clapton as we had in Europe, Britain, and, more recently, the United States. I asked him why he didn't call Scott Cameron.

"Well, I don't want to talk to the Mighty Midget," Forrester said, using the unflattering nickname he had coined for Cameron. What Forrester wanted was for me to talk to Muddy about joining forces for Eric's upcoming tour of Japan. And not only that, they wanted to lock in Muddy for future tours. Forrester said that having Muddy around was good for Eric. Then he went on to say he "wanted" Muddy. It took me a minute to realize what he was hinting at. I never knew for sure, but it sure sounded like he might want Muddy in his own management stable. "Enough of the Mighty Midget," Forrester said.

I met Muddy at the airport in Cleveland on Thanksgiving evening. We were there for a show with soul singer Millie Jackson at a nearby venue, the Front Row Theatre in Highland Heights. In the cab to the hotel, I told Muddy about my conversation with Forrester and he got really upset. "Why didn't Eric's manager call Scott?" I told Muddy that I had put that same question to Forrester. "I'm just the messenger," I said to Muddy. "Other than that, I didn't know anything about it. But I can tell you this, he expressed very clearly to me that he might be interested in managing you. At least that's what it sounded like to me," I added. When Muddy repeated that Forrester had to talk to Scott, I reminded him that the two of them didn't get along. "Scott's my manager, Scott's my manager," Muddy kept saying. I didn't know what to tell him, so I went with the facts. I pointed out that the tours with Clapton had been great for him. That it would have taken him years to play in front of that many people on his own. And it helped sell a lot of records. Muddy agreed, but repeated that Eric's manager was still supposed to call Scott.

I gave Muddy my opinion: I thought it would be best for him to tour Japan with Eric before we ever went over there on our own. Muddy remained upset—with me, with Forrester. He couldn't get past Clapton's manager ignoring Scott and tracking me down instead. So, now I was caught in the middle of this mess just for being the messenger. I tried my best to make Muddy see the bigger picture, but I realized Scott's hold over him was strong.

The upshot was that Eric didn't sit in on the *King Bee* recording, and we did not accompany Eric on the Japan tour. It was a win for Cameron that later began to look like deliberate sabotage—again, just my opinion. Instead Cameron put together a three-city tour of Japan with Muddy as the headliner. I noticed a lot of unsold seats on that tour.

Chapter 38

KOI AND COW TONGUE

We had a few more dates to do after the recording session. The last shows before leaving for Japan would be at one of Muddy's home gigs, Harry Hopes (May 16–18, 1980). On the last night all hell broke loose. We were due to fly to Japan in a few days, yet Muddy and Scott hadn't said a word about how much we'd be paid for the trip. When one of the band members brought it up in the dressing room before the show, Muddy snapped: "None of your business," or something like that.

Given the famously high cost of living in Japan at that time, not to mention the greater distance we would have to travel to get there, it seemed clear that our usual overseas pay package—$600 per week, plus hotels—would be inadequate. Since Muddy, and Scott had failed to come up with a number, the band did: $1,000 per week, plus hotel. That's what they thought would be fair. I had no idea how much the shows in Japan were paying Muddy, but everyone figured they had to be making it worth his while to go.

Our first stop on the tour was Tokyo. Most of the places we stayed on the road were nothing special, but occasionally, we'd be treated to a first-class hotel. The one where we stayed in Tokyo, the New Otani, was one of them.

The grounds were beautiful and peaceful, a real oasis in the heart of one of the biggest cities on earth: ponds, little paths to stroll, bridges and sculpture everywhere. The ponds were stocked with koi, which are colorful fish and sometimes wildly pricey. I'm told they bring thousands of dollars apiece in some markets. I explored the gardens with Pinetop, Willie, Guitar Junior, and Fuzz. The weather was perfect,

Willie fishing in the hotel pond, Tokyo. Photo by Brian Bisesi.

and it was great to be outside. The koi caught Pinetop and Willie's attention. Both of them loved to fish. On the road in the States, especially if we were down south, Willie and Pinetop would try to do some angling. Occasionally they'd get nailed for fishing without a license. But here we were gaping at a fully stocked pond, and no sign of anyone with the authority to bust us. Willie and Pinetop must have thought they'd hit the motherlode. The fish were there to look at, but Willie and Pinetop began fantasizing about getting a fishing rod, catching some of these suckers and frying them up.

I noticed Willie had been eating something as we approached the pond. He still had a little piece of bread in his hand. As he gaped at all those koi, Willie was deep in thought. The wheels were spinning. After a few minutes he had an announcement to make. He knew how to catch the fish. He walked over to the edge of the pond, took what was left of the bread, stuck it in the water and started waving it back and forth. In seconds, every fish in that pond was clustered around Willie's bread, nibbling on it. Willie was very proud of what he had accomplished. "I don't need no fishing rod," he boasted. "I got all the fish I could want right here." As I watched Willie mesmerize the koi with his piece of bread, I could only hope that he wasn't going to try to grab a few in his bare hands.

Feeding them was probably a no-no, let alone pulling them out of the pond to make a fish fry. Squatting by the water, Willie chuckled at his own antics, and the other guys were cracking up, too. Finally, Willie gave it up and let the fish go back to whatever they had in mind before he showed up with his slice of bread. I found out later on that some of those fish were protected by law. You're really not supposed to monkey around with them. Luckily, we were able to get out of Japan without the police in hot pursuit, or a school of fish ravenous for more bread.

The opening act for our first show in Japan was a Japanese blues band heavy into Robert Johnson songs. Muddy was tickled by that. When he heard them playing, he got up from his chair in the dressing room and said he had to see these guys to believe it. He went to the edge of the stage to watch. Since they were singing in English, we assumed that they could speak English, too. Wrong! They spoke not a word of it, we later learned. As a highlight of their show, the band's two guitar players exchanged instruments midway through a song. But instead of handing the guitars to each other, they threw them up in the air and, without missing a beat, caught them and kept on playing. Muddy and the rest of the band got a big kick out of that routine. After they finished their set, the Japanese bluesmen came backstage to meet Muddy. You could tell that they were thrilled, but upon encountering Muddy, they stood silently and bowed. Muddy tried to compliment them about the Robert Johnson songs, but figured out real fast that they had no idea what he was saying. It blew Muddy's mind that they could sing these songs just by echoing the rhythms and intonation of the voice they heard on Johnson's records.

For his part, Muddy always made an attempt to say "thank you" in the local language. Audiences would roar with approval when he responded to a round of applause by thanking them in their native tongue. Sometimes it didn't come out exactly right, like the time in Germany when Muddy attempted to say "danke schön." After being introduced, he stepped up to the mike and came out with "donkey donkey." No crowd reaction at all. Muddy was perplexed and disappointed. He wanted to get it right. When he came off the stage, he asked me again how to say thank you in German. My German wasn't a whole lot better than his, but I coached him a little and the next night he nailed it: "Danke . . . Danke schön." The crowd roared with approval; mission accomplished! Now we were playing East Asia and Muddy asked me if I knew how to say "thank you" in Japanese. I told him to try saying "arigato." I heard Muddy muttering to himself—"arigato . . . arigato"—until he got it right. When he said it onstage on our first night, the crowd shrieked with gratitude. I was happy to have helped Muddy pull it off.

At the end of one show, some Japanese fans who were hanging around in the dressing room offered to take us out to dinner the following night. Jerry Portnoy, Bob Margolin, and I were happy to accept the invitation. We looked at it as a chance to experience Tokyo, with some locals to guide us around. And to top it off, a free dinner! After a brief tour, our three hosts brought us to a hibachi-style restaurant. They spoke English reasonably well and insisted that, since dinner was their treat, they would do the ordering. Sounded good to me! I was looking forward to what I expected would be some meat or fish and vegetables grilled on the sizzling metal dome while we watched. This would indeed be a treat for me—and something of a relief—since I am not a fan of sushi. Our hosts signaled to the waiter that they were ready to order, and proceeded to do so, in Japanese of course. We sat around the dome waiting for our food, making small talk with our new friends. Finally, the waiter approached, platter in hand, with what looked like slabs of raw red beef. Upon closer inspection, the meat looked to have been sliced in a way that resembled a tongue. We asked our hosts to identify the meat. Yup, tongue. Cow tongues, to be precise. There must have been a dozen or more of them on that platter. Bob, Jerry, and I looked at each other. Cow tongues!? This was way out of our comfort zone. Even Jerry, who was probably the most adventurous of us, decided to pass. Nothing was going to keep our hosts from a favorite Japanese delicacy. As we passed the platter back to them, they picked up their chopsticks, grabbed tongues, and threw them on the sizzling dome.

I watched in horror as one of our hosts peeled the smoking tongue from the dome with his chopsticks and began eating it. The other two followed suit. I had lost my appetite when I first spotted the platter of tongues. Now, watching our hosts chomping away on the tongues and smacking their lips, I was nauseated. They were clearly enjoying themselves and, polite as could be, continued trying to get us to sample the meat they found so mouthwatering. Bob, Jerry, and I were giving serious thought to strategies for getting out of there gracefully. We didn't want to insult our hosts, but finally all we could do was excuse ourselves and bolt back to our hotel for something more familiar from room service.

Even though this happened many years ago, the sight of a cow still brings back bad memories of that platter of tongues, and my stomach begins to turn!

Chapter 39

BURSTING BLADDER

On the flight over (from Chicago to Tokyo nonstop, fourteen hours), I had noticed this great big guy whose head was heavily scarred. I kept looking at him trying to figure out what his story was. He had a very strong presence about him, like someone who might be a pro wrestler or something like that. At one point Muddy got up to stretch his legs and check on the other guys, and he also spotted him. "I know who that guy is," Muddy said when he stopped by my seat to chat. "He's a wrestler. I've seen him on TV." Later in the flight, Muddy and the guy passed each other in the aisle and talked briefly. Muddy was right. His name was Abdullah the Butcher and he had appeared on TV.

When we arrived at our hotel, it turned out that a lot of American wrestlers were staying there, too—on hand for an American Pro-Wrestling competition in Tokyo. As we waited for our room assignments, the wrestlers milled around the lobby. I recognized a couple of them: Bob Backlund and Dusty Rhodes. And one of the wrestlers recognized Muddy—Stan Hansen, who would go on to become a world champion. He freaked out when he saw Muddy. "I can't believe it's Muddy Waters!" I heard him say. He seemed thrilled to be in Muddy's presence, and I got the feeling that Muddy was equally delighted to have all these pro wrestlers around. Some of them started to make small talk with us. One guy who came up to me and started talking was none other than Hulk Hogan.

This was before Hulk became a superstar. He told me he had been a bass player from Florida before he became a wrestler and invited me to join him and some of the wrestlers for a drink at the hotel bar.

When I got back from Muddy's show that evening, I took Hulk up on his offer and joined him and his buddies for a beer.

I recognized the huge dude holding court at the table Hulk suggested we sit at: André the Giant, another pro wrestler. The wrestlers were drinking and carrying on and occasionally smacking each other, and I began to wonder what I'd gotten myself into. André the Giant kept ordering drinks for everyone, including me. I had been sitting there a while when I noticed a backlog of four or five beers waiting for me, courtesy of André the Giant. "Drink, drink!" he chanted. Then he called for the waiter to bring the table yet another round! I couldn't drink that much beer, no way, no how. But I didn't want to insult André the Giant by spurning his hospitality. I shared my concern with Hulk Hogan and he responded with a story. André the Giant once drank eighty-four beers in one sitting and didn't get up to pee! Not exactly comforting words, given that after one or two, I was going to need a bathroom real soon. "What about all those beers sitting on the table?" I asked Hulk. He told me there'd be no stopping André the Giant from ordering more but to just drink what I wanted. With that, he excused himself and headed back to his room for the night.

As I got up to go to the bathroom, this huge hand reached across the table and slammed me back into my seat. "Sit down," André the Giant commanded. I obeyed and, to my dismay, he summoned the waiter and ordered another round. I'm dying now. My bladder is about to burst, I've got to use the bathroom so bad, and this seven-foot, five-hundred-pound wrestler who can drink eighty-four beers without peeing will not let me leave.

André the Giant knew he had my attention and started to tell me a story. "If you ever want to smuggle something out of the country," he began, "I will tell you how to do it." I had absolutely no intention of becoming a smuggler, but with this giant wrestler staring at me, I figure I better ask him how to do it. For any current or future smugglers out there, here's André the Giant's advice: "A couple of days before you're going to leave, you get a big fish, the biggest fish you can find. You put it in your suitcase and leave it there. Then you put whatever it is that you want to smuggle in the suitcase. When you get to customs, no one will check your bag. Believe me, no one will check your bag!" I never put that advice to the test. I'd been told that André the Giant was very fond of vodka. After he finished the fish story, he jotted down the name of a Tokyo restaurant and said I should tell them that André the Giant had sent me and that I wanted to drink "the good Polish vodka." I saw no reason to tell André the Giant that I didn't drink vodka.

Finally, André the Giant became distracted by someone else at the table, and I was able to slip away to the bathroom. After relieving myself of several beers, I headed back to the table to thank him for the drinks and to say goodnight. By this time the only people left in the bar were at the table with André the Giant. The waiters surrounded them. They stood by with their hands folded and their heads bowed, a sign of respect. I'm sure it was also a sign that they wished these stragglers would get the hell out of there so they could close the bar. As I said goodnight and thanked André the Giant, he reached out and shook my hand. With fingers like he had, it was like shaking hands with a bunch of bananas.

The next morning I had breakfast with Muddy in the hotel restaurant. And much to my surprise we arrived at the same time as Hulk Hogan and his manager Freddie Blassie. "Classy" Freddie Blassie was a real character, a champion wrestler back in the 1950s and '60s who aged out of competition to become a manager and promoter. Hulk saw me and said hello. Then Blassie recognized Muddy, who also recognized him. Blassie suggested we have breakfast together. Muddy was tickled to be noshing with Blassie, a famous wrestler he had seen on TV. His new role was not putting rivals in a hammerlock, it was promoting an upstart named Hulk Hogan, and he wasted no time touting his virtues. He told us more than once that Hulk was going to be huge, and he was right!

Muddy was like a kid around these celebrities from the world of wrestling, men he had seen on TV. His joy was obvious to me, and I was grateful for it. That breakfast may have been the one highlight of our otherwise mismanaged trip to Japan.

Chapter 40

SOMETHING WEIRD

We're near the end of the tour and I'm in my room at the New Otani. The phone rings. It's Scott Cameron. The New Otani was a huge complex. Muddy and Scott were in a separate wing from me and the band. On our road trips across the States and our tours across the Atlantic, normally I would be at Muddy's side pretty much the whole time. This was different. For one thing, Muddy's wife Marva (a.k.a. Sunshine) was with him, and Scott was along for the entire trip as well. Since my room was a bit of a distance from Muddy's and Scott was nearby, I figured he would address any of Muddy's immediate needs. I also wanted to give Muddy and his wife some privacy. Normally, Sunshine stayed home. This was one of the few times she traveled with the band. My role, I assumed, was to wear my road-manager hat and make sure all the band members were accounted for when it was time to leave for a show, that plus taking care of Muddy's guitar and making sure the setup onstage was correct at the venue.

To get a call from Scott was not unusual. What he had to say came out of left field: He said Muddy wanted me to bring his guitar—the one he called "Hoss"—to his room. Why? "He feels like playing." I'm thinking, he feels like playing? I had been working for Muddy and looking after his guitar for about two and a half years and he had never asked me to bring him his guitar in off hours. Not once. Playing the guitar was for shows, not just to noodle around.

I remembered the time when we got back together after a three-week Christmas break, I took the guitar out of its case to tune it, and Muddy told me he hadn't touched "that thing" since the last time we played. He had actually sounded a little bit worried about whether he'd remember how to do it.

I had no reason to doubt that Muddy totally trusted me with Hoss, and also with a second guitar that ZZ Top's Billy Gibbons gave him in Houston when I first started working with the band. Occasionally when a trip ended, Muddy's two guitars would go home with me, rather than to his place in Westmont. I would bring them back when we hit the road again. In other words, Scott's call didn't smell right to me. Something weird was going on.

"Okay, I'll bring it right over," I said dutifully. It was the last time I'd lay my hands on Hoss. The next day when we got ready to leave, Scott called for a bellhop to tote the guitar to a cab. I wasn't exactly sure what was up. I would find out when we got back to the States.

Chapter 41

INDEPENDENT CONTRACTORS

Scott's attitude toward the band came clear every time one of the guys had some issue or problem going on. "Just remember," he would remind me, "they're all independent contractors who can easily be replaced." That's the mercenary way Scott viewed the band, and it told you everything you needed to know about his priorities. In the end, that's exactly the way it went down. Cameron had been an ally of the Delta bluesmen. He had sued Led Zeppelin and later Chess Records for copyright infringement of music created by Muddy and Willie Dixon. But with the whole fate of Muddy's band in the balance, he declared them again independent contractors—not a band at all—and left them in the dirt.

What was really strange is that when the shit finally hit the fan, Scott notified me with a phone call in which he couldn't stop cackling: "Ha, ha, ha, I guess we won't be needing you anymore. The whole band quit, enough of the tail wagging the dog." As far as I know—as sure as I know my name—nobody quit. Nobody. This part of the story has been written about before, and it is wrong. The guys all stood by their agreement: "You fire one of us, you fire us all." Somehow that got twisted into "They all quit." And that's not true. Jerry Portnoy was fired, that is true. It was not in anyone's plans to quit Muddy. What they wanted was to continue backing him and try to work out their differences. I failed to see the humor in Scott calling to tell me that he had just fired the whole band, including me. When I got off the phone with him, I called Muddy. I asked him what was going on? His answer: "Well, you guys all quit."

The backstory is this: Several incidents had happened just before we left for Japan. I can recall three in particular leading up to this debacle. First, Scott had presented the band with the new pay scale that had created dissension in the ranks. Second, right up to the night before we left for Japan, the band had no idea how much they were going to get for the trip. Third, a reliable source had told Jerry Portnoy that he was going to be fired as soon as we got back. To their credit, the guys in the band decided this was unacceptable and stood by Jerry. The consensus view was that Scott was behind all of these changes.

Okay, as all those empty seats made clear, Muddy was not well known in Japan at that time, which is why I thought it would have been better to go there first with Clapton. Without Clapton as the headline attraction, it would take an extra effort at promotion to fill our venues. That was beyond Cameron's skill set. But it wasn't like money fell short of what was needed to pay a hard-working band what they were due. As the tour ended, Scott took me into the hotel's safe-deposit vault and gave me the money to meet payroll. My jaw dropped to the floor when I saw the stack of hundred-dollar bills. It was more hundreds than I had ever seen in my life, but it wasn't all going for payroll.

The band told me to stay out of it. You work for Muddy, they told me. You're Muddy's guy. You two got your own thing going on, so stay out of this. They didn't want me to get hurt. Muddy's beef was that I should have told him about dissension among the band members, what the guys were saying to each other. No way. I had lived and traveled with these guys all over the world. I loved and respected each and every one of them as much as I loved and respected Muddy. It was a lose/lose situation. By talking I was screwed; by not talking I was screwed.

"So, Mud," I said, "now I'm supposed to be your stool pigeon?" What he said next really hurt me. He told me that I would have been next in line for the guitar chair if and when it opened up. "You know that guitar chair was yours." I told Muddy that what I wanted was for everyone to sit down, talk, figure this out, and move on. Muddy would have no part of it. "No, no, they all quit," he stubbornly repeated.

In fact, what they had agreed to do was stick together. If Scott fired Jerry, he had fired all of them. Pinetop Perkins, who probably trusted Scott about as far as he could throw a piano, was, I believe, the last person Muddy thought would leave him. The band had been together for more than seven years and traveled countless miles. I had been there for about two and a half of those years and saw firsthand the bonds among the musicians. They didn't always agree about everything—who does?—but the band members were always there for each other. I clearly saw that, and I do believe they thought my job with Muddy was not in jeopardy. They were wrong!

I couldn't resist reminding Muddy of something he had said to me a few weeks earlier when we were in Canada together. I was in Muddy's hotel room after a gig, counting the evening's take and doing the payroll for the band. As Muddy sat down, his chair collapsed and he started to fall backwards. Fortunately, I was standing right behind him and was able to catch his head before it hit a nearby table. He looked up at me and it was the only time I ever saw fear in his eyes. He thanked me for catching him before he got hurt, and told me he didn't know what he would do without me. I wanted him to remember those words because I do believe he really meant them. I knew I had his attention now and so I tried to reason with him again. I reminded him that he knew me well, that I had always been straight up with him, but now I was being fired.

I didn't know what my future would hold. I needed a gig. I knew Bob Margolin was ready to go out on his own, and the rest of the guys could regroup as the Legendary Blues Band. I figured Guitar Junior would go that way. Was that an option for me? I called Jerry Portnoy. I looked up to Jerry like he was an older brother. Like brothers, we bumped heads sometimes, but we had always been there for each other. Not this time. He told me no, they were getting guitarist Duke Robillard (formerly of Roomful of Blues). Now I felt completely screwed times two, first by Muddy and then by the band. Right after my call with Jerry the phone rang. It was Guitar Junior. He wanted to know if I was going with the Legendary Blues Band. I told him, no, Duke was going with them. Junior was surprised that they weren't taking me. He figured Jerry and I were tight, since we used to room together on tours. Junior asked me to come out to Chicago and put a band together with him. So I packed my bags and headed back to Chicago to play with Guitar Junior.

Chapter 42

REST IN PEACE

I didn't see Muddy again for about a year. One night while Junior and I were in New York for some gigs, I noticed Muddy was playing at the Beacon again. Junior and I wanted to see him, so we went to the hotel where Muddy and the band always stayed. We were hoping we'd have a chance to talk. I also had some strings that I had been meaning to give him. I called Muddy's room and he answered the phone. I told him Junior was with me and that we would like to see him. He said, no, he was napping. I told him I had some strings for him and he instructed me to leave them for him at the front desk. Signing off, he said why don't you two come on down to the show tonight?

Muddy had left tickets for us at the box office. At the end of the show he called out our names. "Two guys are here that used to work for me: Guitar Junior and Brian Bisesi." After the show Junior and I went backstage. Muddy looked really tired. He was sitting in a chair resting and comedian and blues satirist John Belushi was kind of bugging him. Belushi wanted to go out on stage and soon did. He cued the band to play "Sweet Home Chicago," trivializing a blues classic in a way that infuriated Junior. "I should go out there and tear his asshole up for doing that," Junior muttered to me. "He's got no business walking out there like that."

Muddy chatted briefly with me and Junior. He asked what we were doing in New York. "We're working," Junior answered. To which Muddy said, "Oh, well, that's good. You guys, you know that's good."

And that's the last time I ever saw Muddy Waters. I never got a chance to sit down and clear the air. Given half a chance, I still believe I could have helped patch things up between Muddy and the band.

Ultimately, it was a failure to communicate—combined with the bad advice Scott Cameron gave Muddy, lots of it.

By the end of the so-so Japan tour that Cameron had arranged, Muddy's health was becoming more of an issue. I knew about his high blood pressure. What I would learn later on was that heart disease was setting in and Muddy was also dealing with lung cancer. Scott only worsened things by insisting that Muddy dump his old friends, some of the best blues artists in the world, and bring in a new band. The new guys were mostly players he had no history with. It put Cameron in a situation he could now totally control, but Muddy had to work that much harder to hold things together. Muddy had a saying that I heard him repeat many times: "It don't take but one to fuck up a band—more than one, even Crazy Glue can't hold that together." This is not to say he had weak players in his new band or that they were messing up, but they changed his sound enough that he had to be the glue that held it all together. He was playing more guitar than I had ever heard him play before. He had to do that to get the powerful sound he wanted. And then suddenly the sound ended, once and for all.

When I got the news, I was living in New York's Chelsea district, with the woman I would eventually marry. A couple of weeks after Muddy turned seventy, in April 1983, he died in his sleep, at home in Westmont. I took it hard. I was torn apart. This legendary musician had changed my life and given me a career that would sustain me for decades. But along with my gratitude, learning he was gone meant I would never have the chance to work out the differences between him and me—and him and the band—that I knew we should and could have overcome. The sound was going to last forever even if the musicians who played it so well were scattered to the wind.

Chapter 43

AFTERMATH

Muddy slammed the door shut upon our return from Japan the first week of June 1980. An amazing few years with him had launched my career as a professional blues player. Now it was time to pick up the pieces and move on.

I was very grateful that Guitar Junior asked me to come back to Chicago to put together a band that he would be leading. Muddy had coached me on the stuff you've got to watch when dealing with club owners and promoters, and I was up for the challenge. That schooling and the fact that Muddy always thought Junior could make it on his own, gave me the courage I needed to get this thing going. We soon hit our first roadblock.

Word had quickly spread throughout Chicago that Muddy had dumped his entire band. When I called clubs in the immediate area, no one would touch us. Muddy's name was that powerful in the Windy City. I'm not saying he was telling clubs to blackball us. It was just that respect for Muddy was so great that no one quite dared to be the first to hire someone from his former band and risk pissing off the blues legend. Our only option, I decided, was to get out of town, hit the road and hit it hard. And that made for a second snag: finding musicians who would travel with me and Junior.

I started making calls to clubs in the Northeast and throughout the Midwest and was able to string together some dates. Unfortunately, they would not happen for a few months. It was June, the beginning of summer, and clubs were already booked through Labor Day. To make matters worse, as if things weren't bad enough, several of the club owners wanted to include Muddy's name in the advertising for the dates (which I had already decided against). When I informed Guitar Junior of the requests, I was relieved to learn that we were on the same page. Junior wanted to make it on his own name, not Muddy's. I respected his decision not to ride Muddy's coattails. I'm sure Muddy appreciated that, too.

On the upside, a May 1980 recording session Junior did with some of Muddy's band (Pinetop Perkins, Calvin Jones, Willie Smith, me on guitar, and Joe Berson on harmonica) was soon to be released as part of Alligator Records' *Living Chicago Blues, Volume VI*. It would also mark the first time Junior's name would appear as Luther "Guitar Junior" Johnson on a record. This disc would prove to be very helpful to me as I continued to book gigs. Now we had a fresh product that I could send to clubs.

By September, we finally had everything together and headed out. First stop: Niagara Falls, New York. Toby Rotella, a good friend of Muddy's entire band, had just opened a club there, the Imperial Garage. This would become a regular stop for us in the coming months and into the New Year.

I was wearing many hats helping keep Guitar Junior on the road: booking agent, manager, guitar player, road manager, and relief driver. I was beginning to wonder what I had gotten myself into. Trying to wear all of those hats—dealing with some new crisis on a daily basis while trying to keep my sanity—had me harking back to Victoria Spivey's warning five years earlier. "So you want to be a musician?"

Life on the road involves a lot of downtime in hotels. Some musicians like to watch TV, play cards, read. And some like to drink. After a couple of months on the road, Guitar Junior and I discovered how two of the guys in the band were spending their time. On an off day, this might not be a problem, but when there's a gig that night: problem. This was a four-piece band and half of it was now visibly drunk onstage. The final straw came one night at a club in Newport, Rhode Island. It was a venue that had been very good to us. We had played there several times and packed the place wall to wall. As Guitar Junior was introducing the band, the drummer passed out drunk just as his name was being called. Junior glanced back at him and added these words to his introduction: "And he's a fired motherfucker." As I came off the stage the woman who booked the club immediately approached me. She had witnessed this horror show from a ringside seat. I figured she would tell me to clear out and never come back. Much to my surprise, I was told Junior and I were always welcome to play there—but not the other two guys in the band. I dreaded what lay ahead, a few more gigs with these guys and the long drive back to Chicago. I was quickly learning how hard it can be to keep a band together. Unfortunately, Junior and I had no instruction manual to guide us through this latest fiasco. Upon arriving in Chicago, the first order of business was to find replacements for our rhythm section.

Since our work was mostly east of Chicago, Junior figured it made sense to find a drummer and bass player from the East Coast—my home turf, so of course the task fell to me. I picked up the phone and called two players I knew would be dependable and easy to work with: Ola Dixon and Michael "Mudcat" Ward, both of them wonderful people and great musicians. The only questions: Were they interested? And were they immediately available? Finally, a stroke of good luck (or so I thought). Both of them had just left Johnny "Clyde" Copeland's band and were looking for work. They agreed to meet us at our next scheduled date, New Year's Eve (1980–81) back at the Imperial Garage in Niagara Falls.

As Guitar Junior and I left Chicago, he began to feel sick. By the time we arrived at the venue to set up he was really sick. Toby, the club owner, informed me that they were expecting a full house—four to five hundred people. Ola and Michael arrived shortly after we did. Junior was under the weather, but everything was going to be all right, I thought. Wrong again. I was learning that there was always another "level to the basement." Junior announced that he was too sick to play and wanted to go to the hotel immediately.

We would have to do the gig without him, our star attraction. I delivered the bad news and watched jaws drop. What to do? Well, as the saying goes, there's no business like show business! The show must go on. I was so lucky to have Ola and Michael there. They weren't happy about the situation, but they were real pros. We put our heads together and came up with a plan. Ola volunteered to do the bulk of the vocals, Michael agreed to sing a few songs and I would contribute some instrumentals on the guitar. We were winging it, but the club owner had no choice. It was too late to try to find another band on New Year's Eve so he had to depend on us to pull it off. Somehow, we made it work. The next morning, I brought Junior to the emergency room at a local hospital. It looked like a bad case of the flu. Unfortunately, there would be no time for him to rest and recover because we had to leave immediately for our next date, ironically—back in Newport, Rhode Island.

I continued working with Guitar Junior for the next year and into 1982. By then we finally had an agent booking dates for us, one less hat I had to wear. But it was getting to the point where Junior and I needed a break from each other to maintain our friendship and our mutual respect. The constant stress I had endured over the previous two years had finally caught up with me. On a break between gigs, I went home to see my doctor to ask about a persistent pain in my gut. He told me I had an ulcer. Yes, it was time for a change.

I was living in New York City at that point and settled for working locally, plus the occasional date backing Philadelphia-based harmonica great Steve Guyger. Finally, for the first time since the fateful day when I joined Muddy on stage in that New Jersey club, I had only one hat to wear: guitar player.

In April 1982 I got an unexpected call from the Boston-area booking agent now handling Guitar Junior's dates, Paul Kahn of Concerted Efforts. J. B. Hutto, the Chicago slide-guitar master, needed a guitar player ASAP. Any chance I'd be interested? Oh, yes, there was! I was told to meet J. B. that weekend at The Haunt, a club in Ithaca, New York. I had played The Haunt before with Junior so I was familiar with it—a great room that drew a very lively crowd.

Our accommodations were in the club owner's home. I was greeted at the front door by Hutto himself. Pretty much the first words out of his mouth were to ask if I was hungry? I said I was. "Good, let's go," he said. He had a restaurant in mind that was near the club and apparently he wanted company.

I didn't really know J. B. I had seen him play a few times, the first of them about about six years earlier in Boston. The second time was when he opened for Muddy at a Seattle club in 1978, when I was filling in for Guitar Junior. As we settled down at our table, out of the blue J. B. said to me, "I want you to know, you got the gig." I told him I thought he should hear me play with his band before offering me the job. His response floored me: "No, you're one of Muddy's boys, you got the gig." I repeated my view that he should hear how we sounded together before offering me the job. "No, you're one of Muddy's boys, you got the gig." It was the first but not the last time I would hear that from a musician I respected. After playing with J. B. that night, I gladly agreed to join his band. I would have stayed with him forever. J. B. was a lot of fun. He was an easygoing guy who treated his band very fairly. Unfortunately, cancer ended his life a little over a year later, in June 1983.

The great ones were starting to go.

A month earlier I had been in Chicago for Muddy's funeral. Shortly after learning about Muddy's passing, on April 30, I received a call from Bob Margolin asking me if I would like to go to the funeral with him. I very much wanted to be there to pay my respects to a man I loved who had changed my life forever. Bob and I worked out the logistics for the trip. Coincidentally, he had a gig already booked at our friend Toby Rotella's Imperial Garage. The plan was for me to fly to Buffalo. Bob would pick me up at the airport, and we would continue on to Niagara Falls, pick up Toby, and drive straight to Chicago. I wanted to send flowers to the funeral home before I left, so I took care of that and made my plane reservation.

When we picked up Toby, he thought it was best to take the "shorter route" to Chicago by way of Canada. From my past experiences crossing into and out of Canada with Muddy's band, I fully expected that border agents would mess with us. And sure enough, coming out of Canada and into Michigan the agent raised an eyebrow after asking to see ID and noticing that everyone in the

J. B. Hutto. Courtesy of Brian Bisesi.

van was from a different state. I guess he smelled trouble. So did I. I had seen this movie before. When he asked what all of us from different places were up to, Bob Margolin, at the wheel, replied: "We are going to Muddy Waters's funeral." To my surprise (and relief) the agent waved us through, no problem.

Once we arrived in Chicago, we secured hotel rooms for the night. I wanted to stretch my legs after the long drive so I headed out of the hotel for a walk around the neighborhood. A few minutes later, I bumped into Paul Oscher, Muddy's former harmonica player. Paul had already been to the viewing earlier that day and talked a little about the scene at the funeral home. The line of mourners extended way down the street, he said.

In Memory
of

McKinley Morganfield
(MUDDY "MISSISSIPPI" WATERS)

WEDNESDAY, MAY 4, 1983
VISITATION: 7:00 P.M.   FUNERAL: 7:30 P.M.

METROPOLITAN FUNERAL PARLORS, INC.
4445 South King Drive ● Chicago, Illinois

REV. C. W. HOPSON, Officiating

Program from Muddy's funeral.

The next day we all went to the funeral home to be with Muddy one last time. When I entered the building, I was greeted by Scott Cameron, Muddy's manager, who led me over to where Muddy lay at rest. He wanted to show me that he had placed the flowers I sent right up front, next to Muddy. It was an act of kindness to me and I was touched by it. We stayed for the service, then headed back to Niagara Falls for the scheduled club date. It felt good to play with Bob again that night as we paid tribute to Muddy and his music.

For the next couple of years I continued to play mostly around New York City with two of Paul Oscher's former bandmates, Ola

Johnny Ace, Ola Dixon, and me, New York City. Photo courtesy Brian Bisesi.

Dixon on drums, and my old pal Johnny Ace (Acerno) on bass. We became the house band at a Manhattan club called the Abilene café, where we backed up blues greats including Pinetop Perkins, Jimmy Rogers, Guitar Junior (all former Muddy sidemen), Johnny Littlejohn, Hubert Sumlin (both former Howlin' Wolf sidemen), early Sun Records piano great Rosco Gordon, and many others.

I reunited with my old friend Louisiana Red (Iverson Minter) in the late nineties to record two albums for Earwig Music. These sessions were very special to me, because I was surrounded by some of Chicago's best blues musicians. As the sessions unfolded, I asked some of the guys how they wanted to approach a song we were about to record and was shocked by their response: "You're one of Muddy's boys, how do you want to do it?" Some of these guys had previously worked with Albert King, Little Walter (Jacobs), and Albert Collins and here they were, deferring to me? I was both uncomfortable and honored that my association with Muddy had earned me such esteem among musicians I deeply respected.

Louisiana Red (left) with Charles Otis. Photo by Brian Bisesi.

A few years later I was able to put together a session for Louisiana Red in Woodstock, New York, with my lifelong friend Jimmy Vivino (bandleader on Conan O'Brien's late-night talk show), who was living there at the time. He brought Levon Helm and Garth Hudson, formerly of The Band, to the studio. Together Jimmy and I produced what would become *A Different Shade of Red: The Woodstock Sessions* for Severn Records. And just as Levon had done for Muddy in 1975, he arranged for Louisiana Red to receive Woodstock's key to the city.

The following year, 2003, Jimmy and I would team up again to produce an album for Muddy's son Big Bill Morganfield, *Blues in the Blood*, a Blind Pig recording. And several years later I would work again with Bob Margolin coproducing Big Bill's album *Born Lover* for Black Shuck/Vizztone.

While the Morganfield session was unfolding, Bob and I both felt that we had created a musical setting in which Muddy would have felt quite comfortable. We were happy to make that happen for his son Bill; the vibe was there.

After my time with Muddy, I've always tried to approach every gig I did, every session the same way: if Muddy were to walk into the

Big Bill Morganfield. Photo by Brian Bisesi.

studio or club right now, what would he think? Would he like what he was hearing? Would I be making him proud?

By the turn of the twenty-first century after basing myself at times for work in NYC, Chicago, Atlanta, San Francisco, and Philadelphia, my wife and I opted for a quieter life on the outskirts of Philly. The endless grind on the road had taken a toll on me. The hotels, the airports, the road food, hauling equipment, driving, pay that had not really changed since I first started in this business decades earlier were all factors in that decision.

I had no regrets. I had been privileged to spend my entire adult life as an itinerant blues musician. The work with the landscaping company, the outfit I quit in 1978 to join Muddy's traveling roadshow on the fateful drive to Nashville, was the last day job I ever had. All these adventures flowed from the accident of being in that New Jersey club a couple of days after Luther "Guitar Junior" Johnson slipped on the ice in Boston and Muddy Waters invited a dazzled twenty-something to fill in.

More than once I heard Muddy say this: "When you work for me, you wear that for life." Little did I know when I walked into that Jersey club on a cold March night many years ago that Muddy would take a chance on me. Thank you, Muddy Waters, for giving me my livelihood, my path forward in music. Yes, I will proudly wear that for the rest of my life.

ABOUT THE AUTHOR

Photo by Ann Bisesi

Brian Bisesi went on from his years as a road manager and designated guitarist with Muddy Waters to a career as a performing musician spanning nearly forty years. From homes in New York City and San Francisco, he toured throughout Europe, Canada, and the United States with blues masters Luther "Guitar Junior" Johnson and J. B. Hutto. He also toured with Muddy Waters's son Big Bill Morganfield, among others. *Blues Explosion*, recorded with Hutto, won the 1984 Grammy for Best Traditional Blues Album. *Got to Find a Way*, a recording made with Luther "Guitar Junior" Johnson, was nominated for a Grammy in 1988. Bisesi also coproduced a recording made in Woodstock, New York, with Louisiana Red featuring Garth Hudson and Levon Helm, alumni of Bob Dylan's legendary group The Band. Of his work with Morganfield, Bisesi remarked: "At one point Bill's band included Kenny 'Beedy Eyes' Smith, son of Willie 'Big Eyes' Smith. It was strange being on the bandstand with Morganfield and

Smith, because I had played with both of their fathers. I was the youngest player in their fathers' bands. Now I was the oldest!" Bisesi lives with his wife in Bucks County, Pennsylvania, and has contributed articles to the magazines *Big City Rhythm & Blues* and *Rhythms* (Australia).

Made in United States
North Haven, CT
13 March 2024

49968702R00124